CONTENTS

PART: ONE
Tracing
Lines & Shapes
to Learn
Pen Control
28 Pages

PART: TWO
Number Tracing
22 Pages

PART: THREE
Math Practice
Counting, Adding
Subtracting
Matching & More...
50 Pages

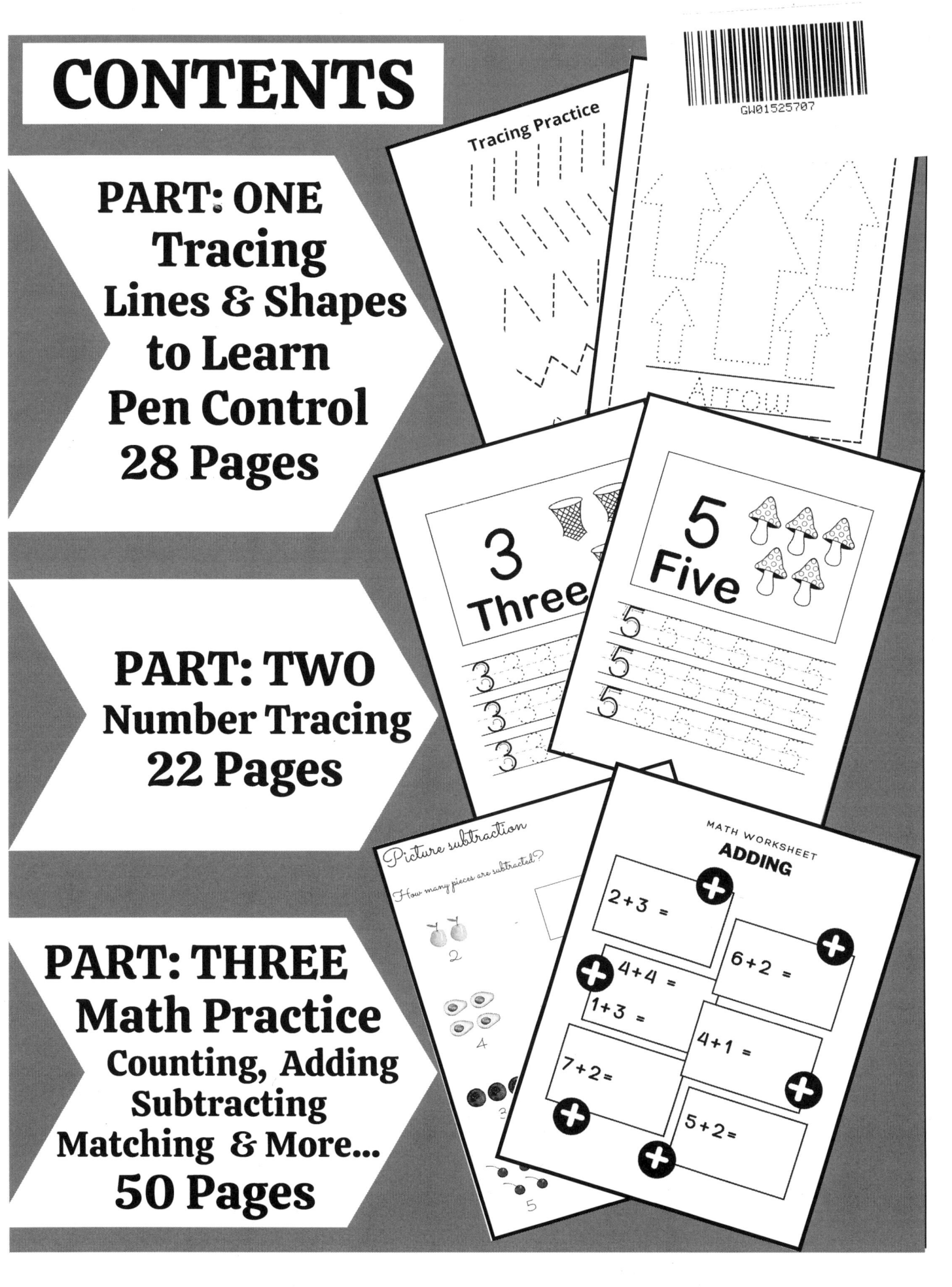

This Learning Book Belongs To

....

....

Thank you for purchasing this book. If you found this book helpful, then feedback on Amazon would be greatly appreciated. Your feedback matters.

Tracing Practice

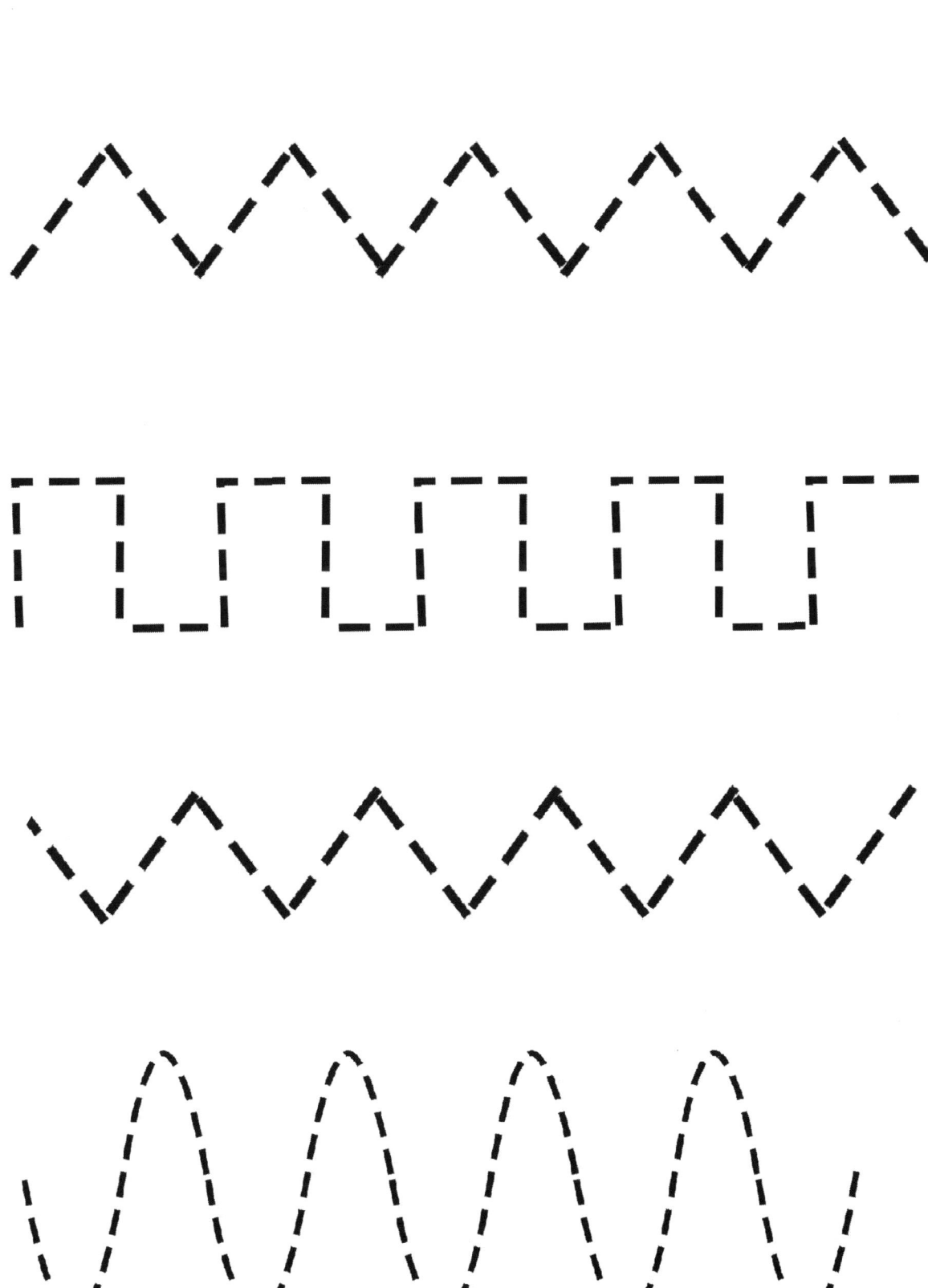

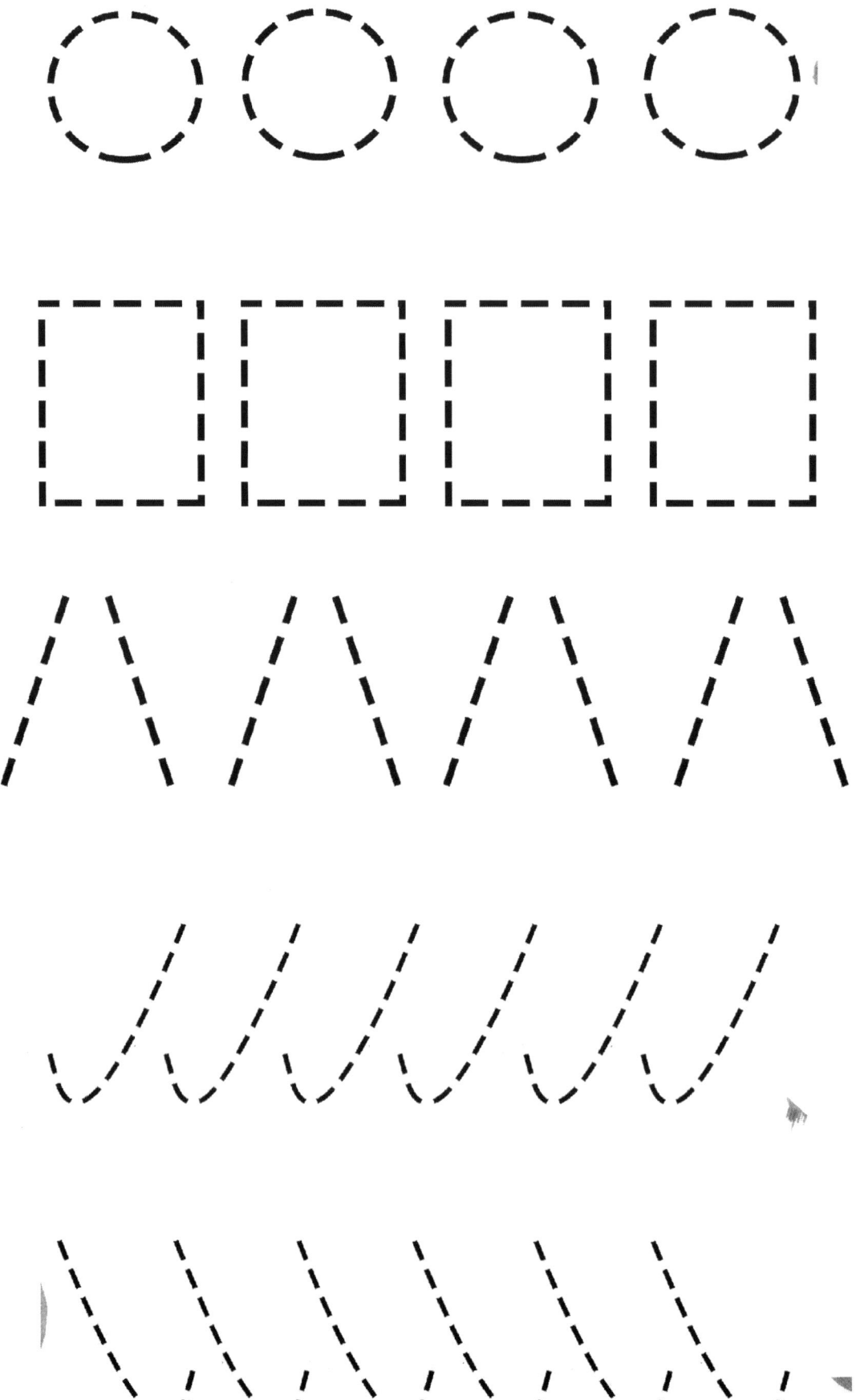

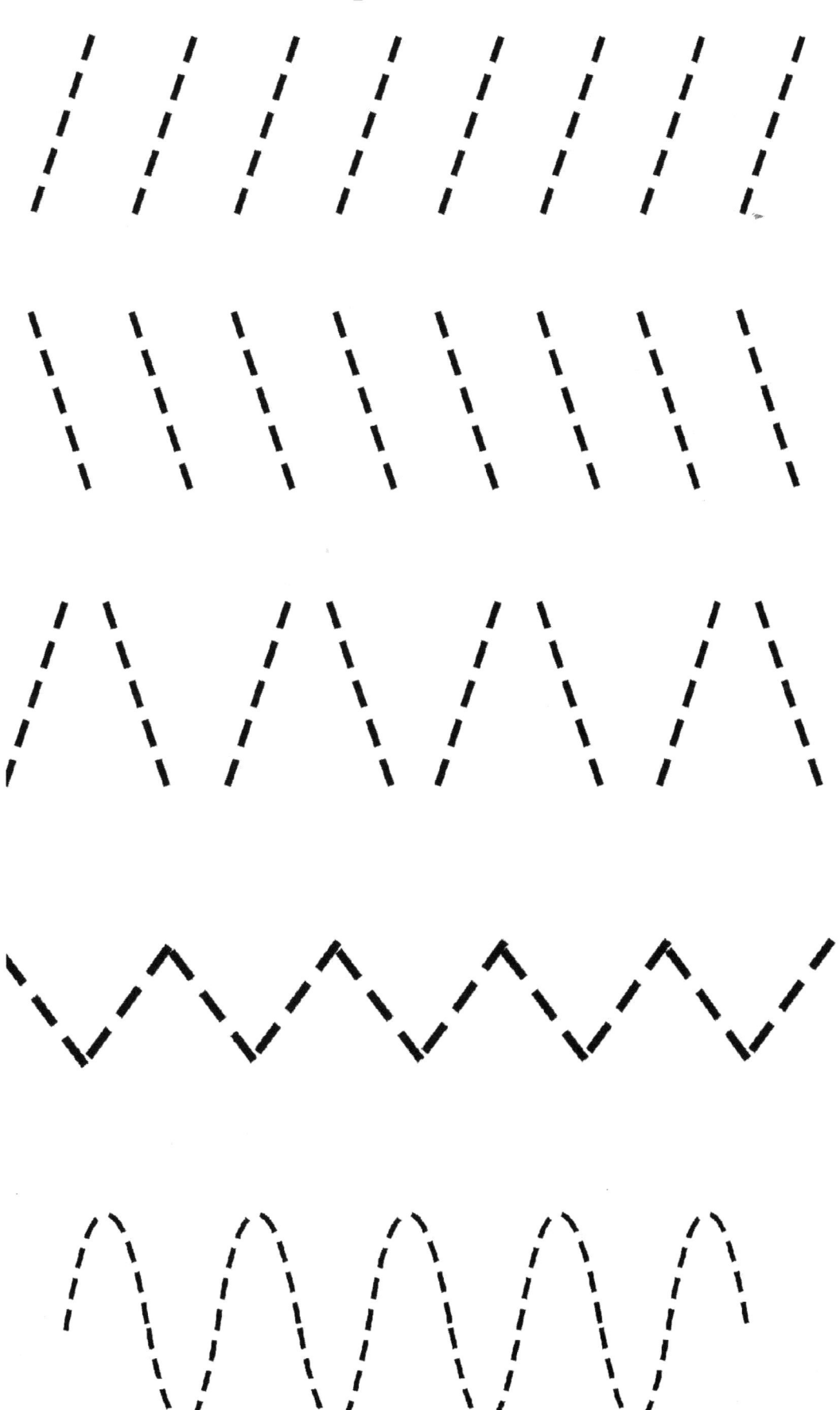

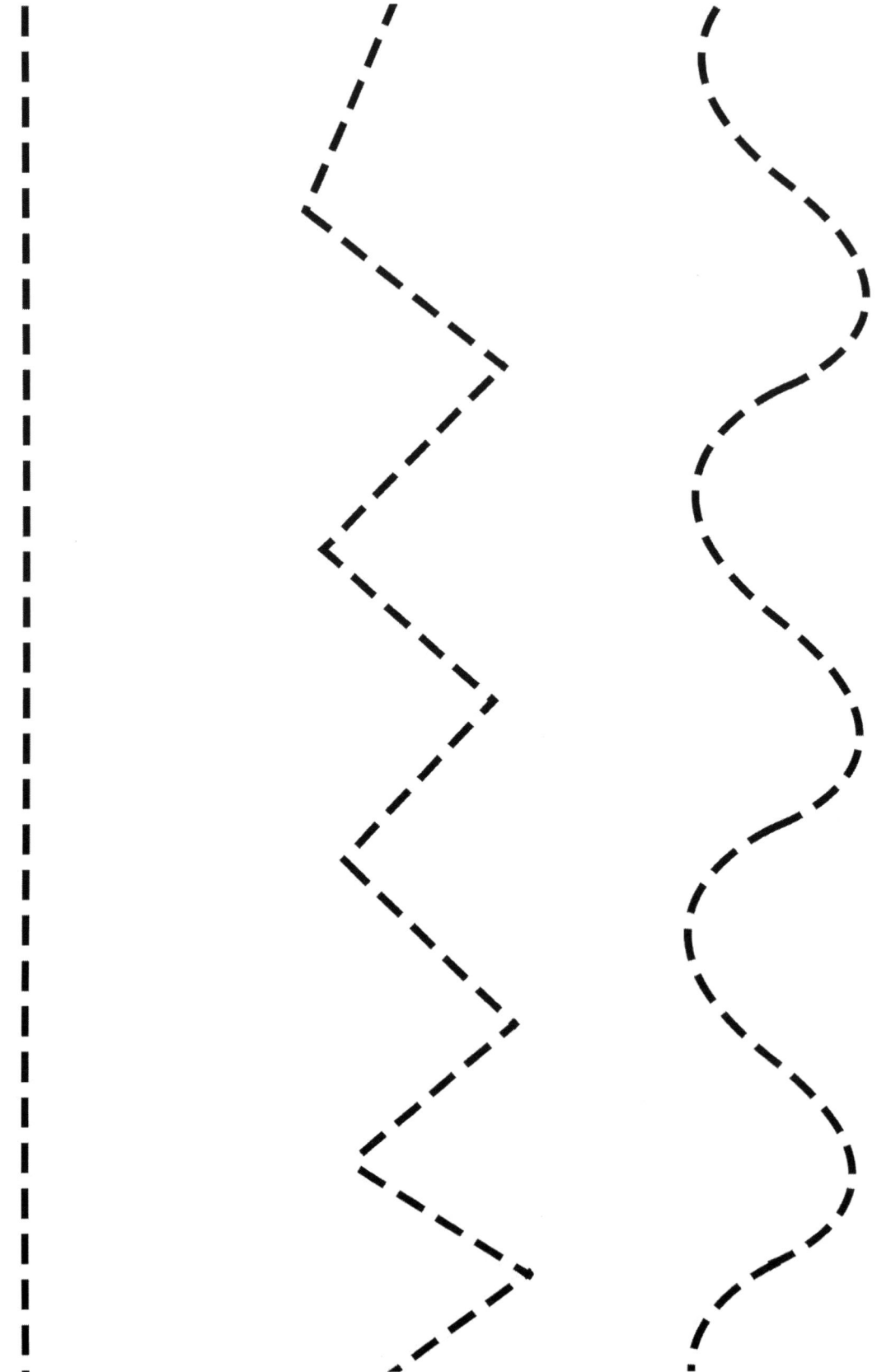

Tracing Shapes

Name: ───────────────

Rectangle

Name: _____

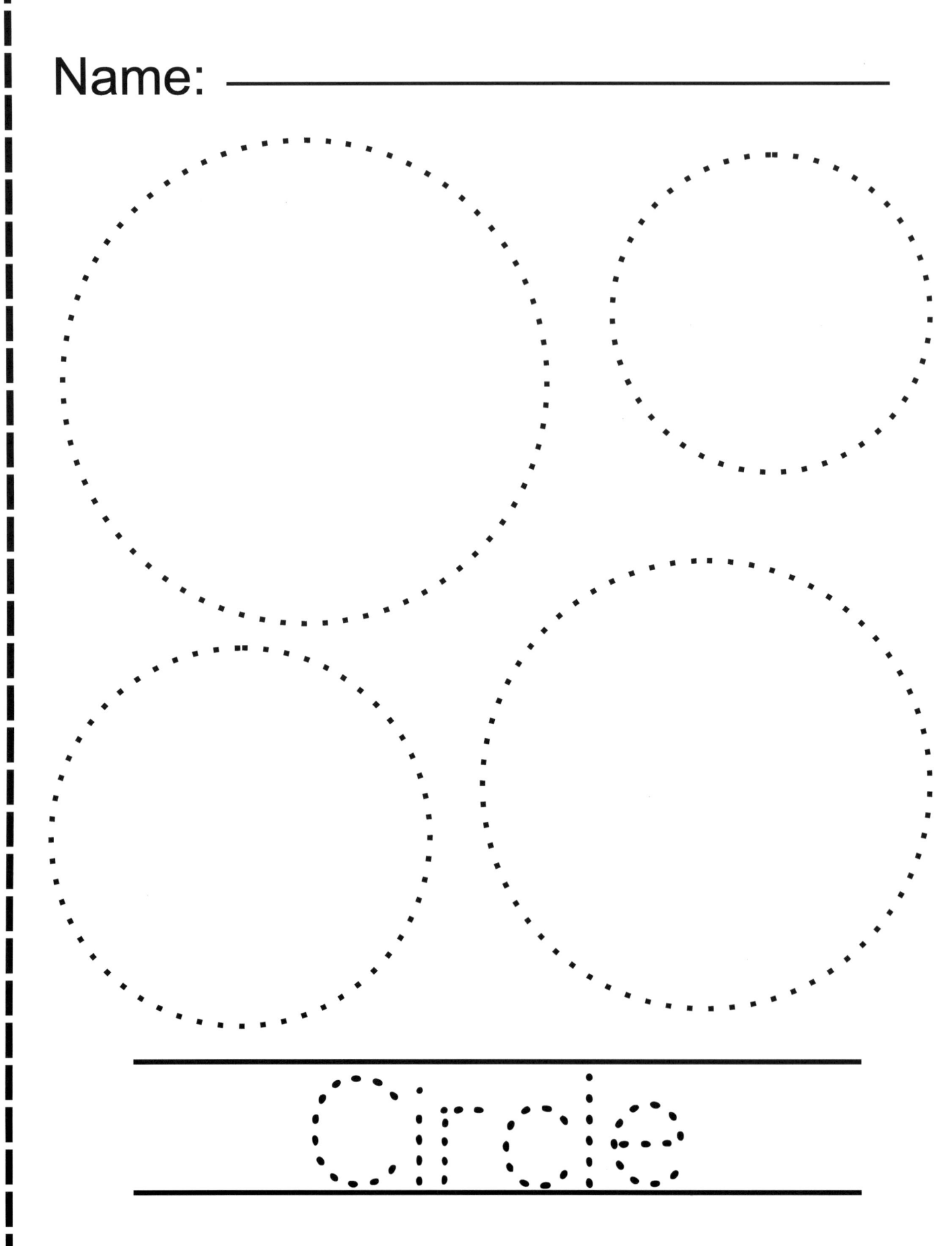

Name: ——————————————

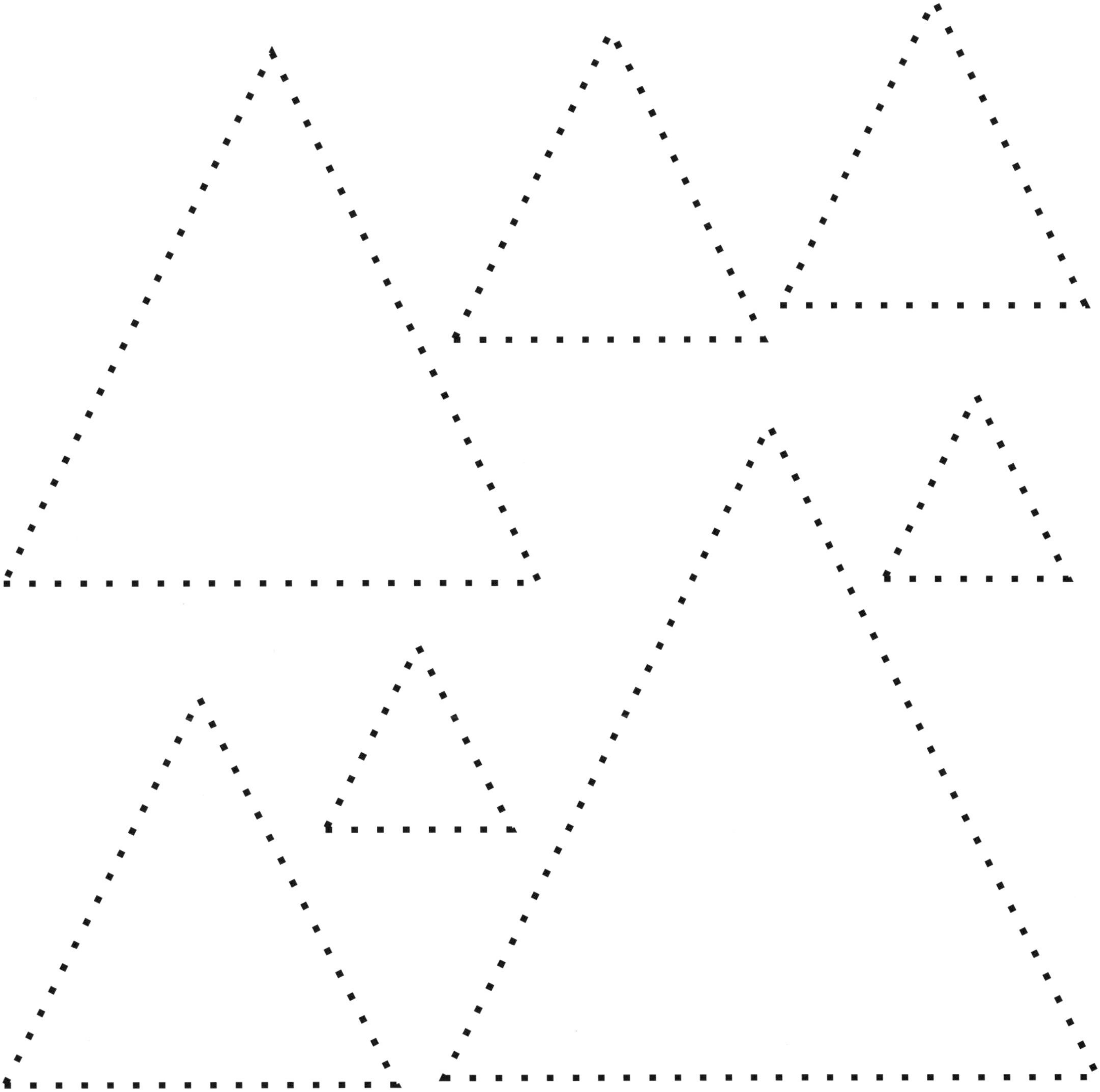

Triangle

Name: _____

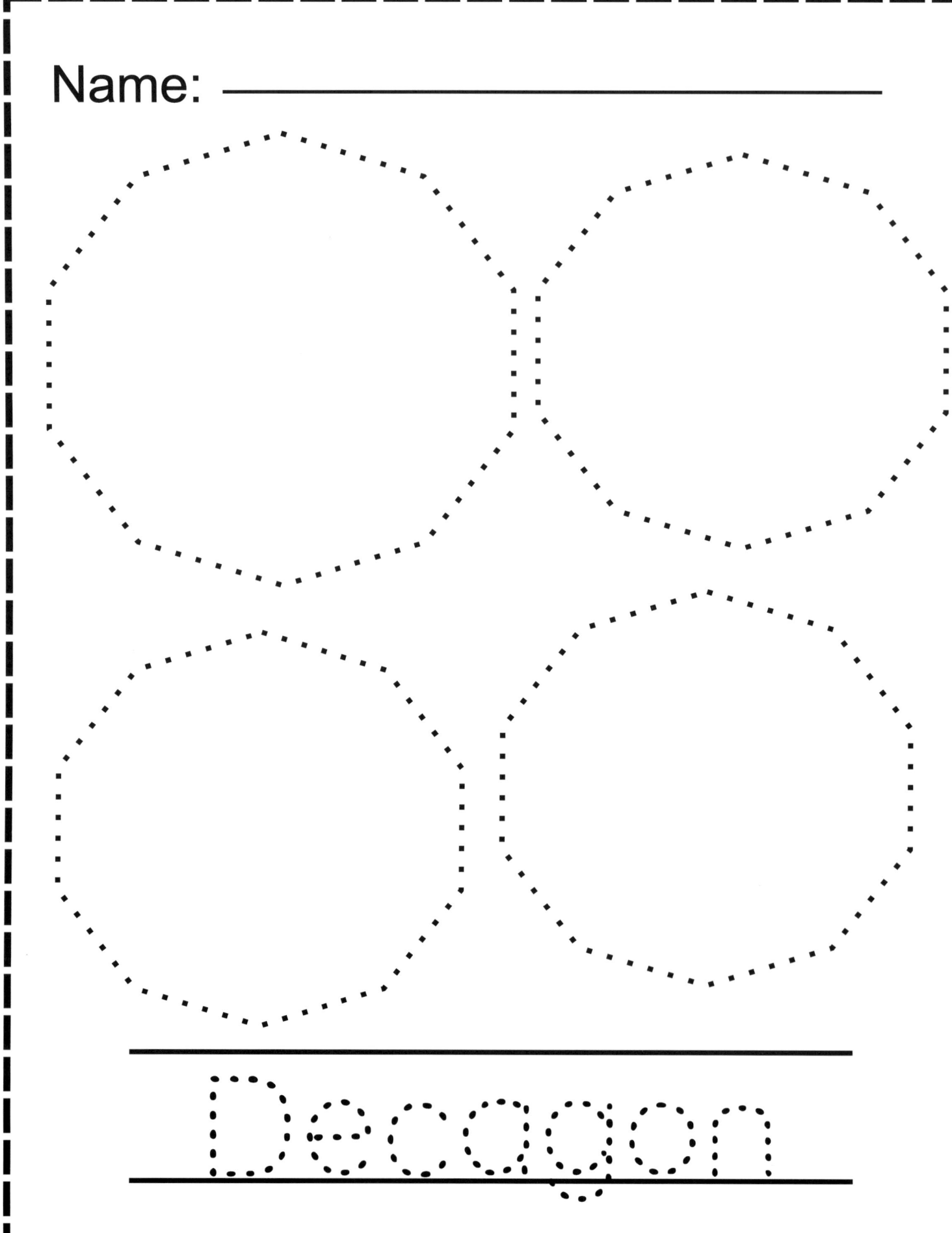

Decagon

Name: ─────────────────

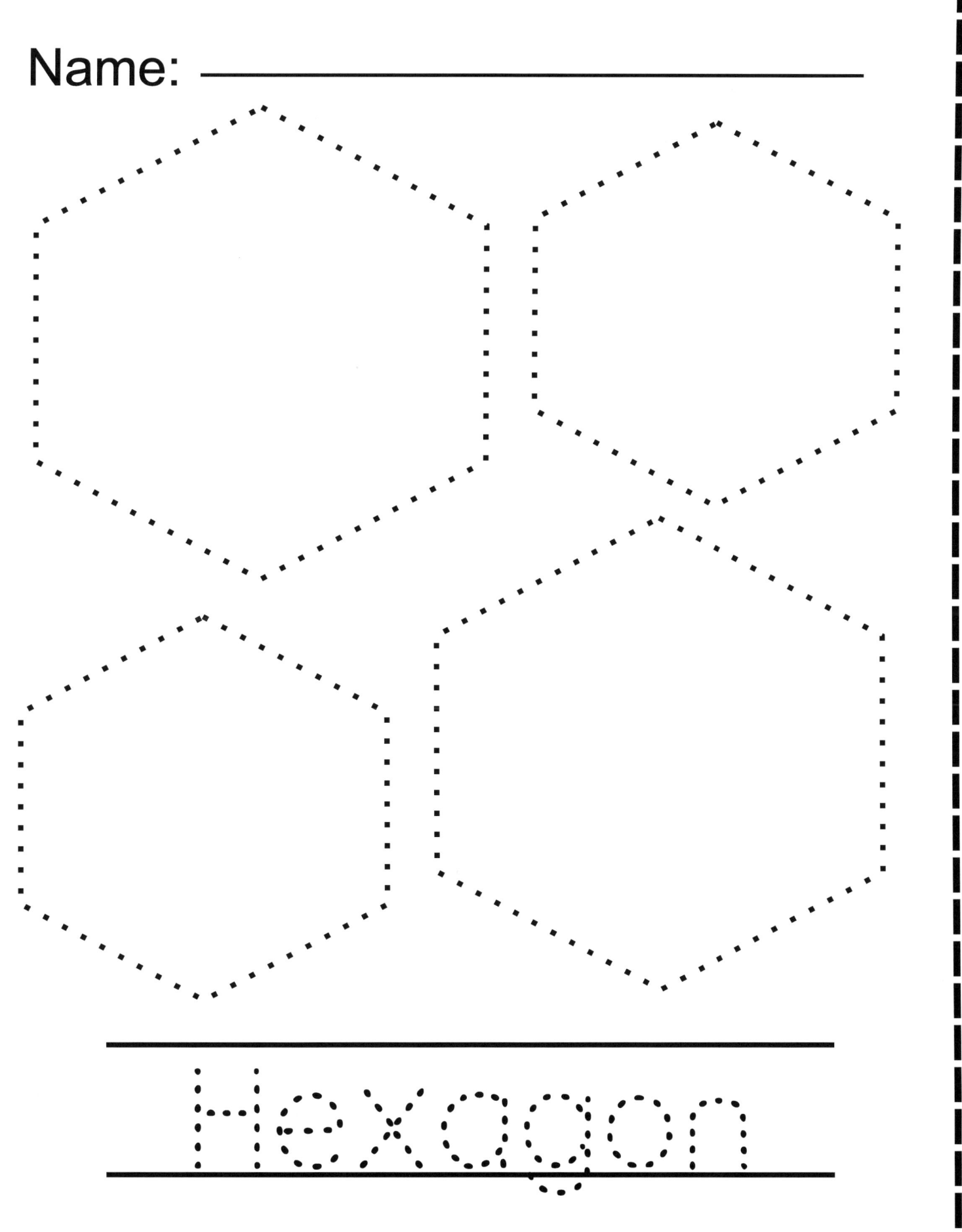

Hexagon

Name: _____

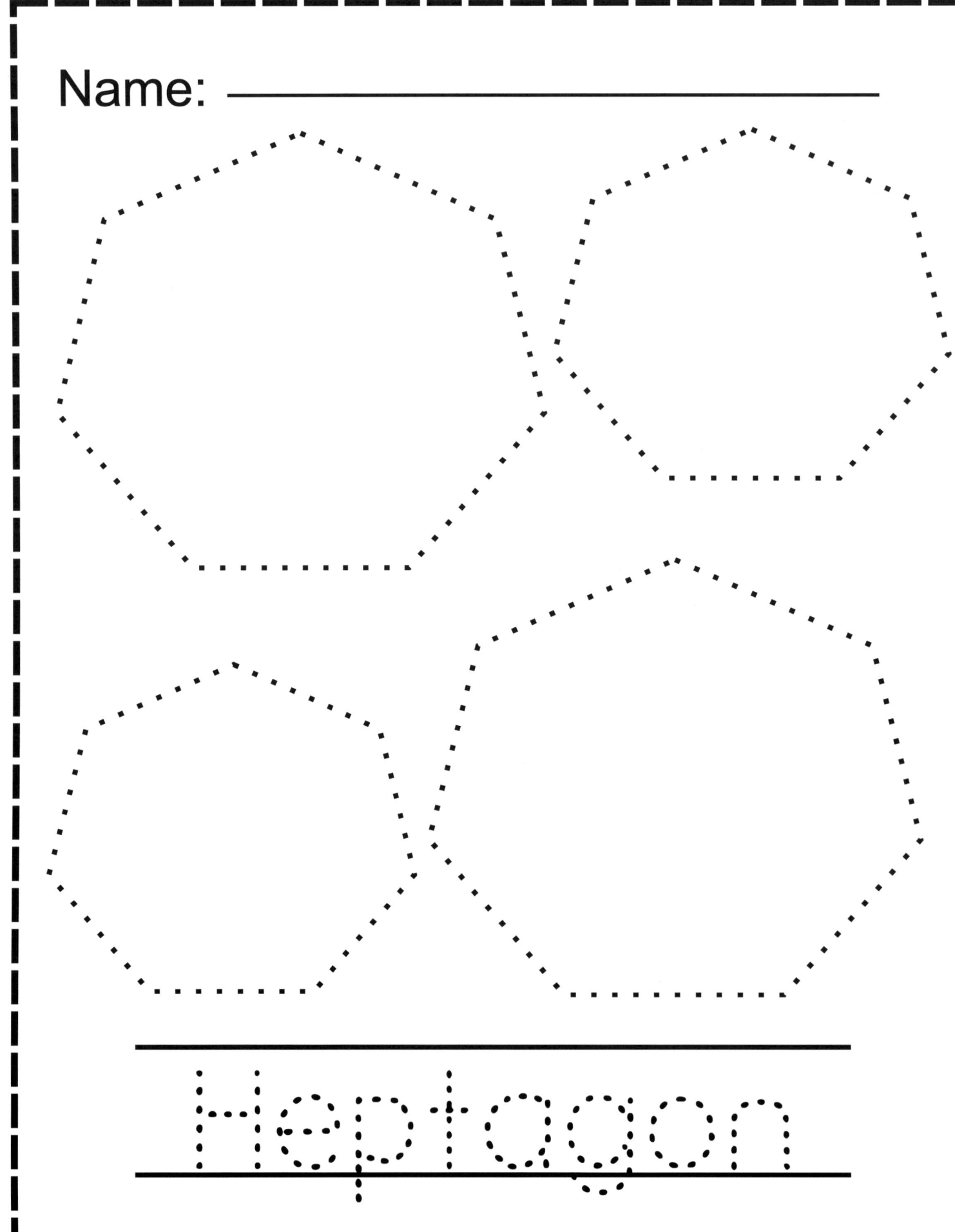

Heptagon

Name: ───────────

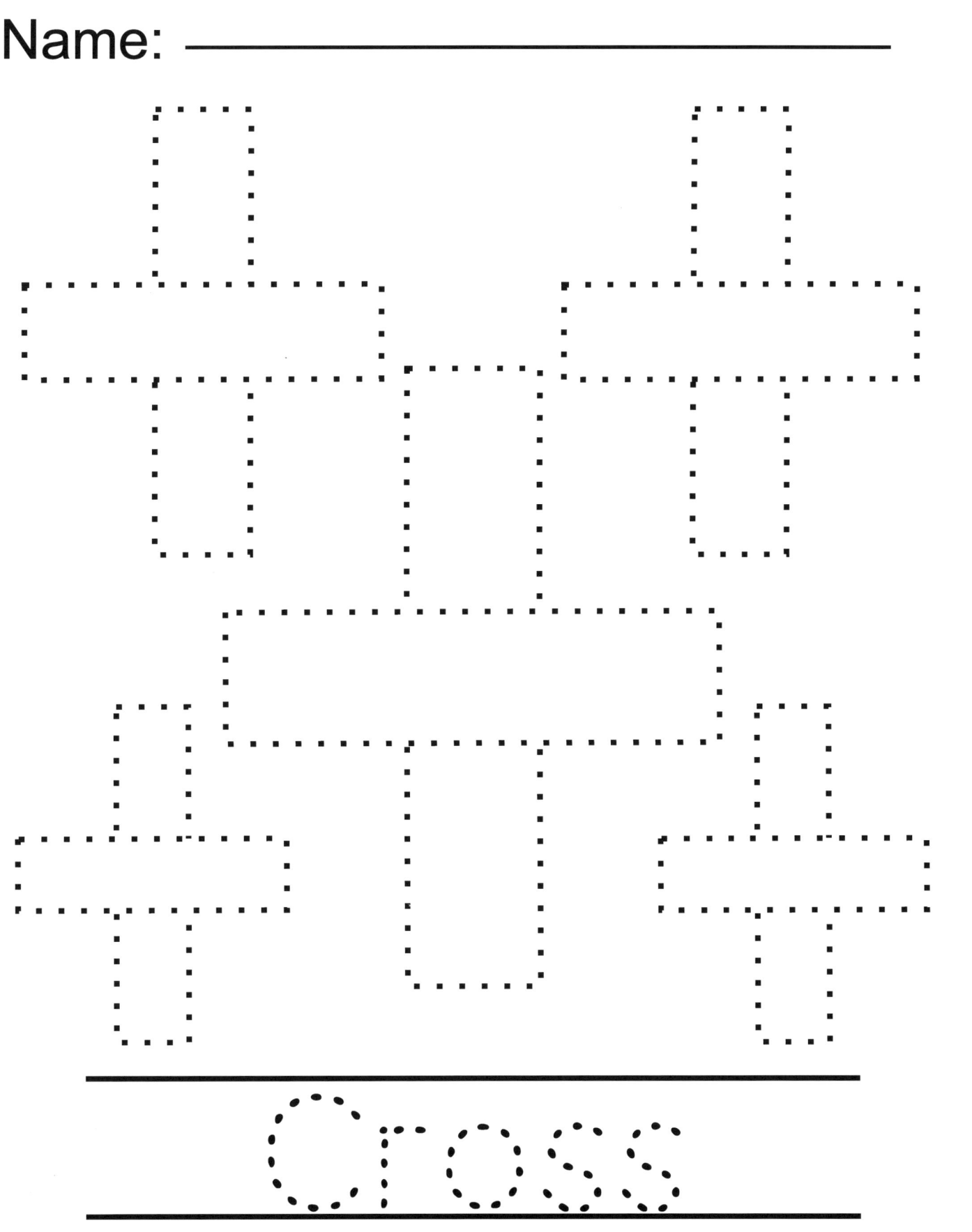

Cross

Name: ─────────────────

Arrow

Name: _____

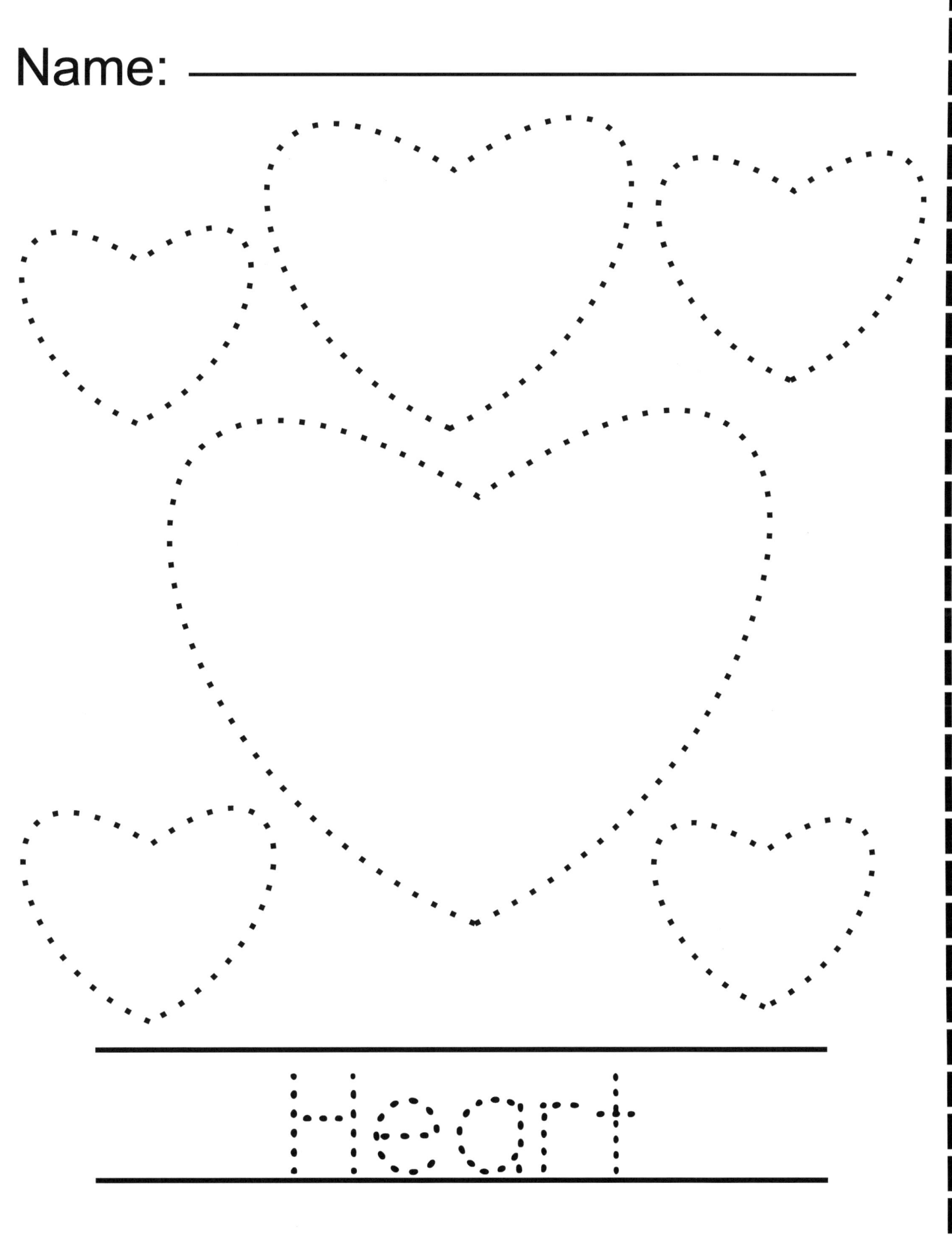

Name: _____

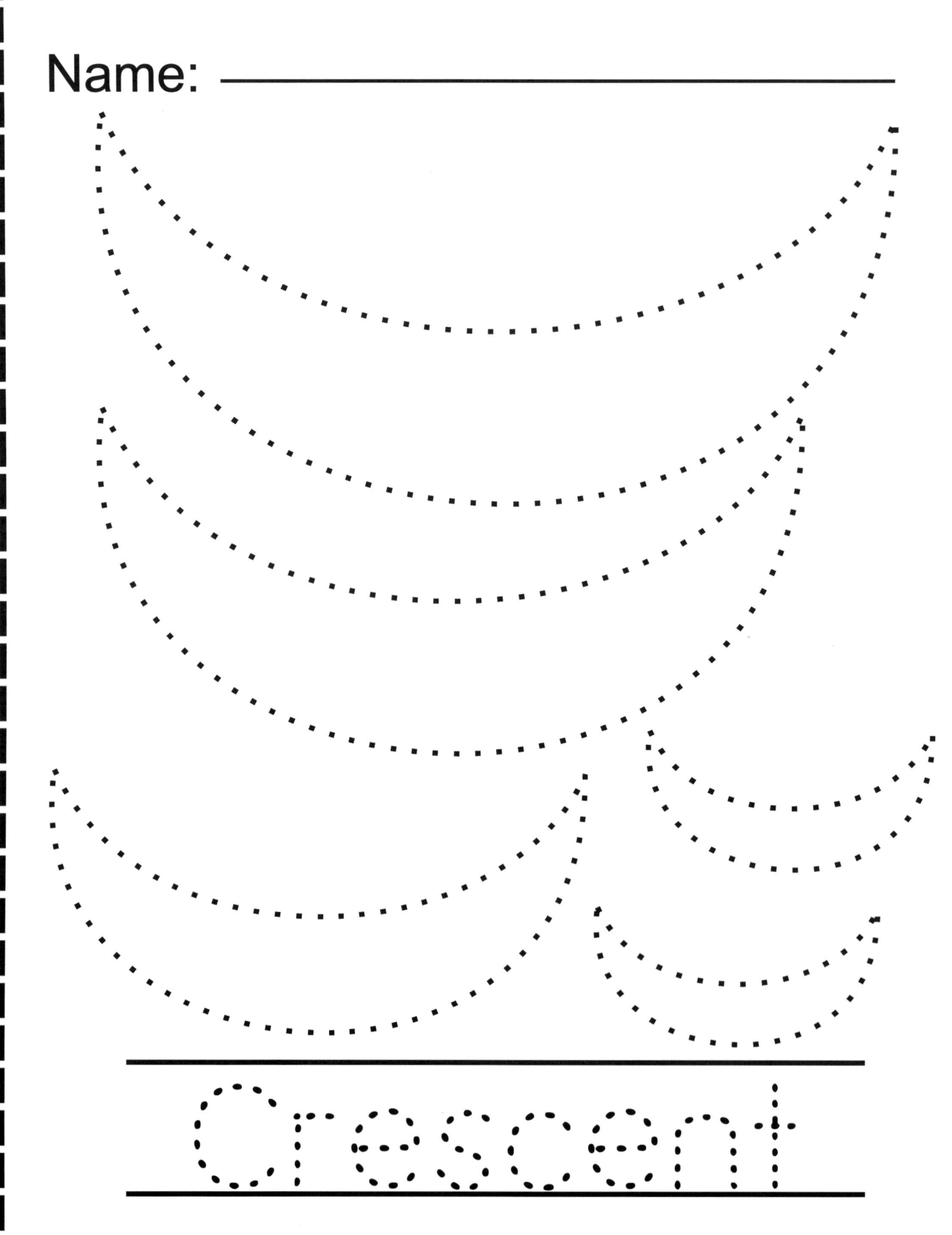

Crescent

Name: _____

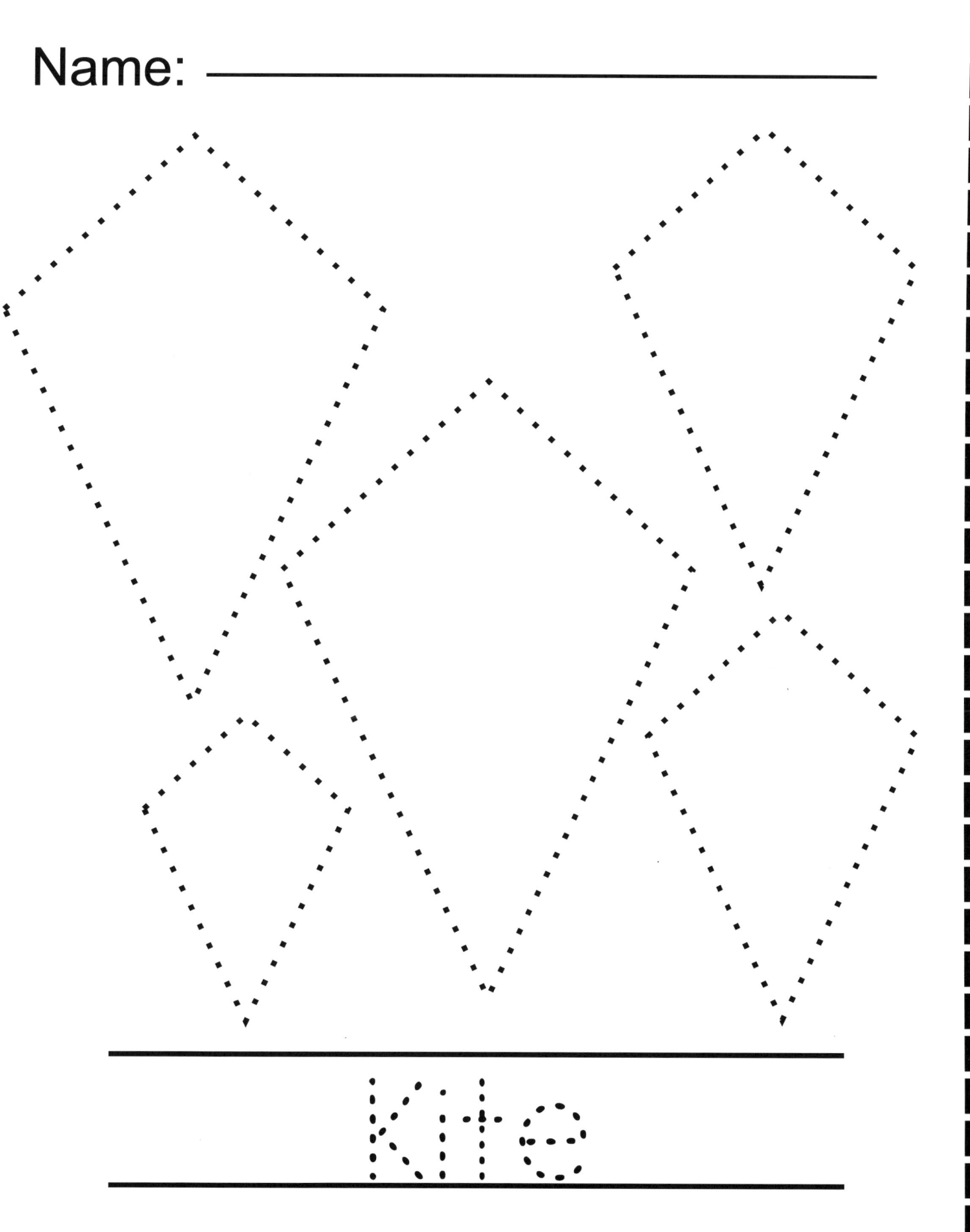

Kite

Name: _____

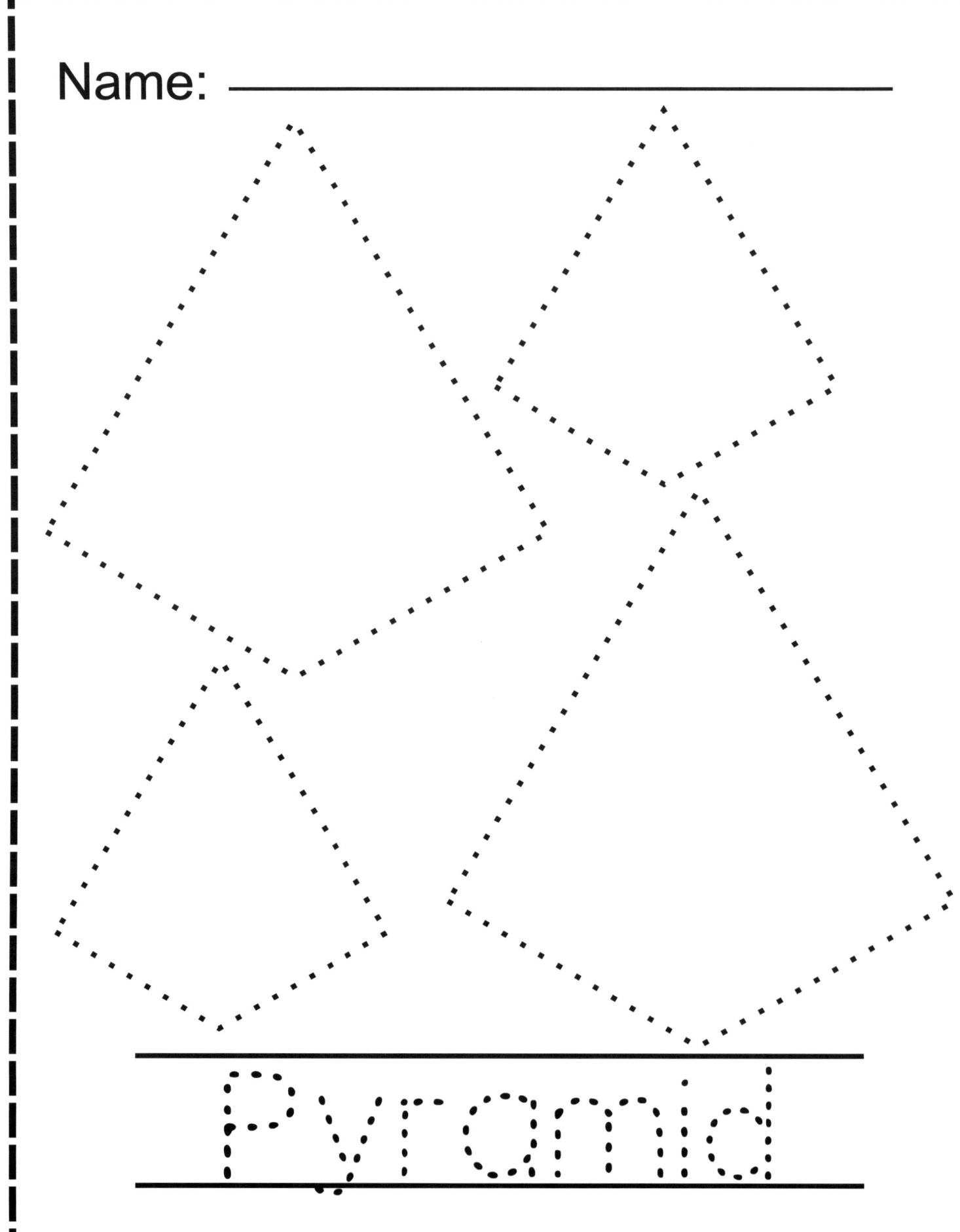

Pyramid

Name: _____

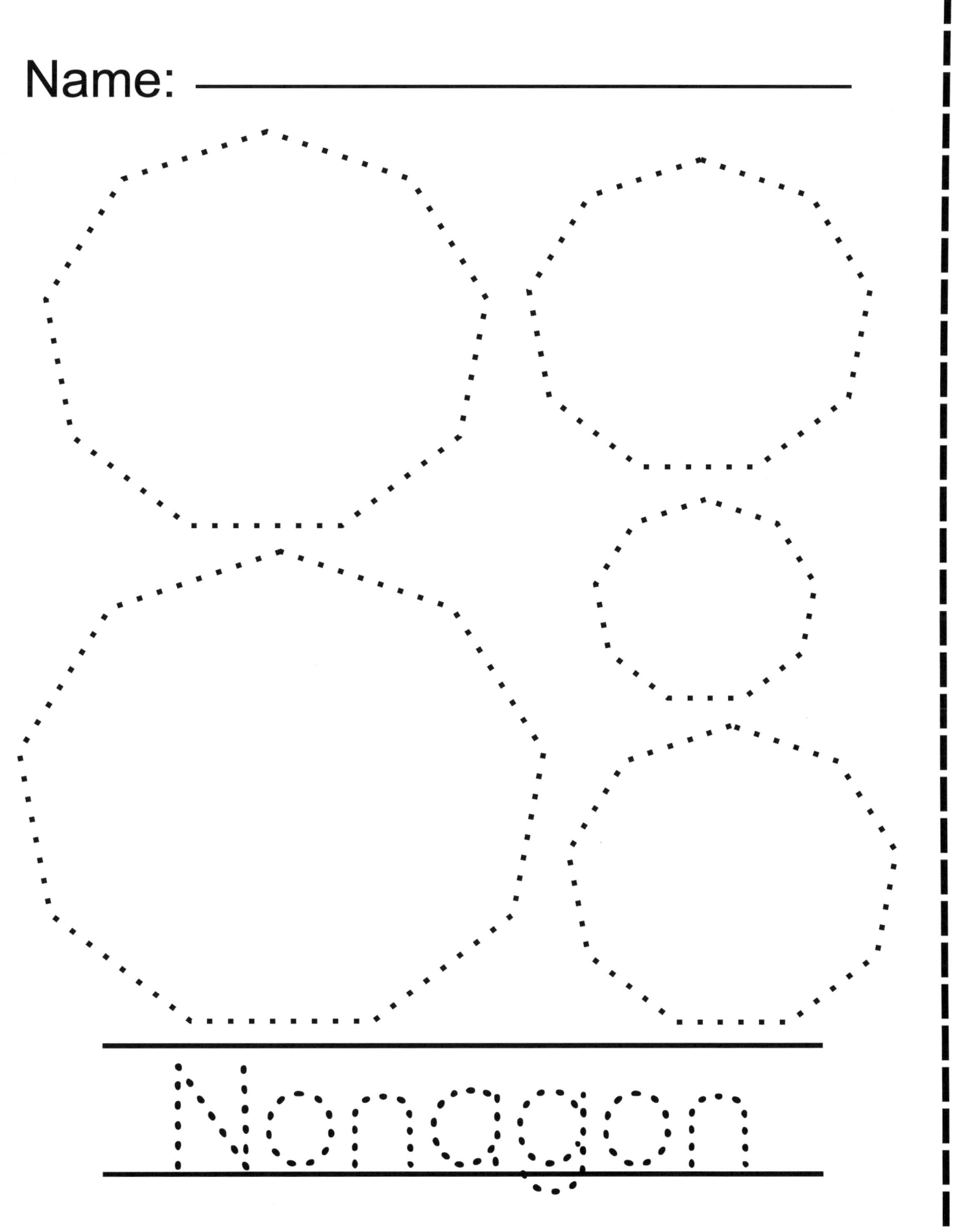

Nonagon

Name: _____

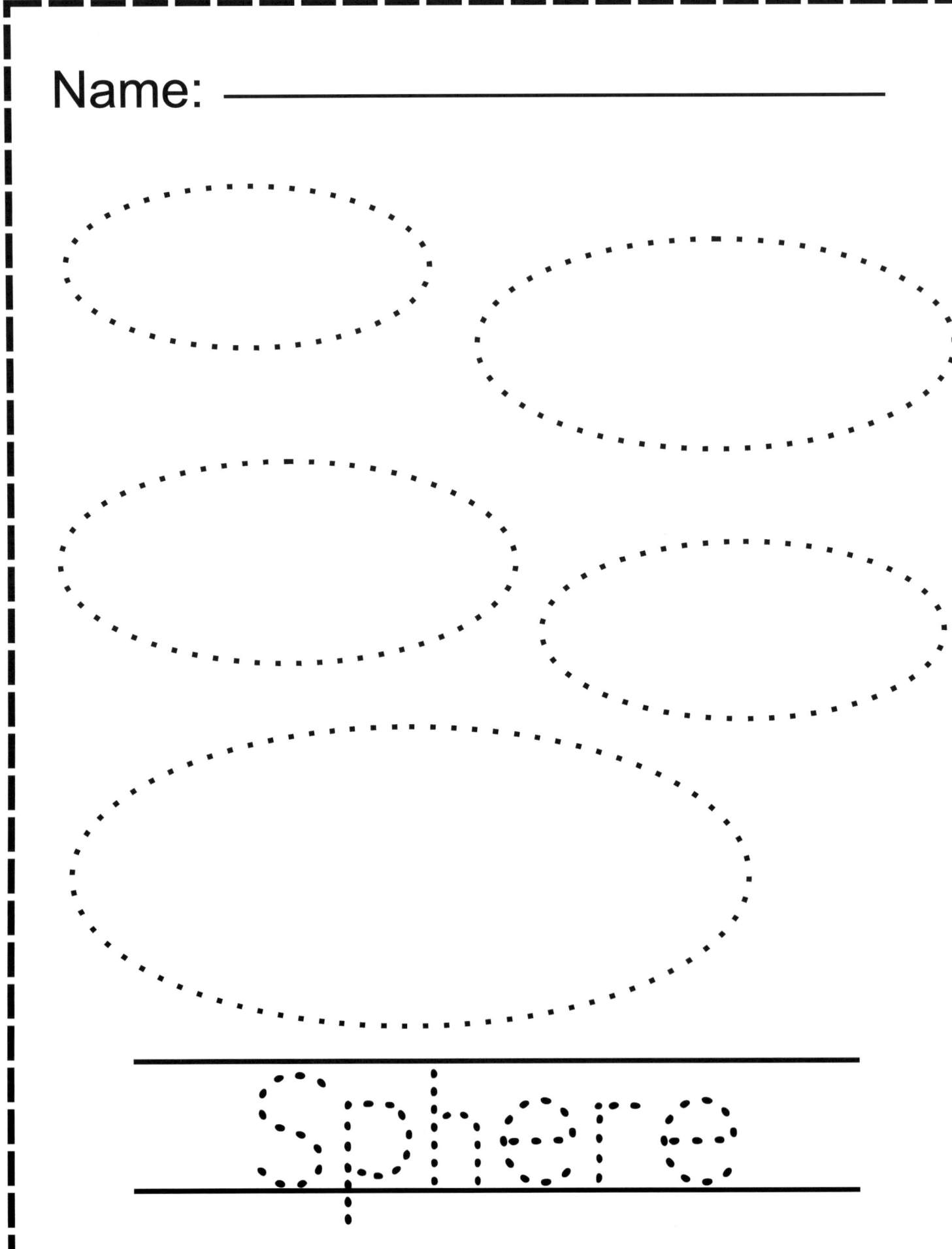

Sphere

Name: ───────────────

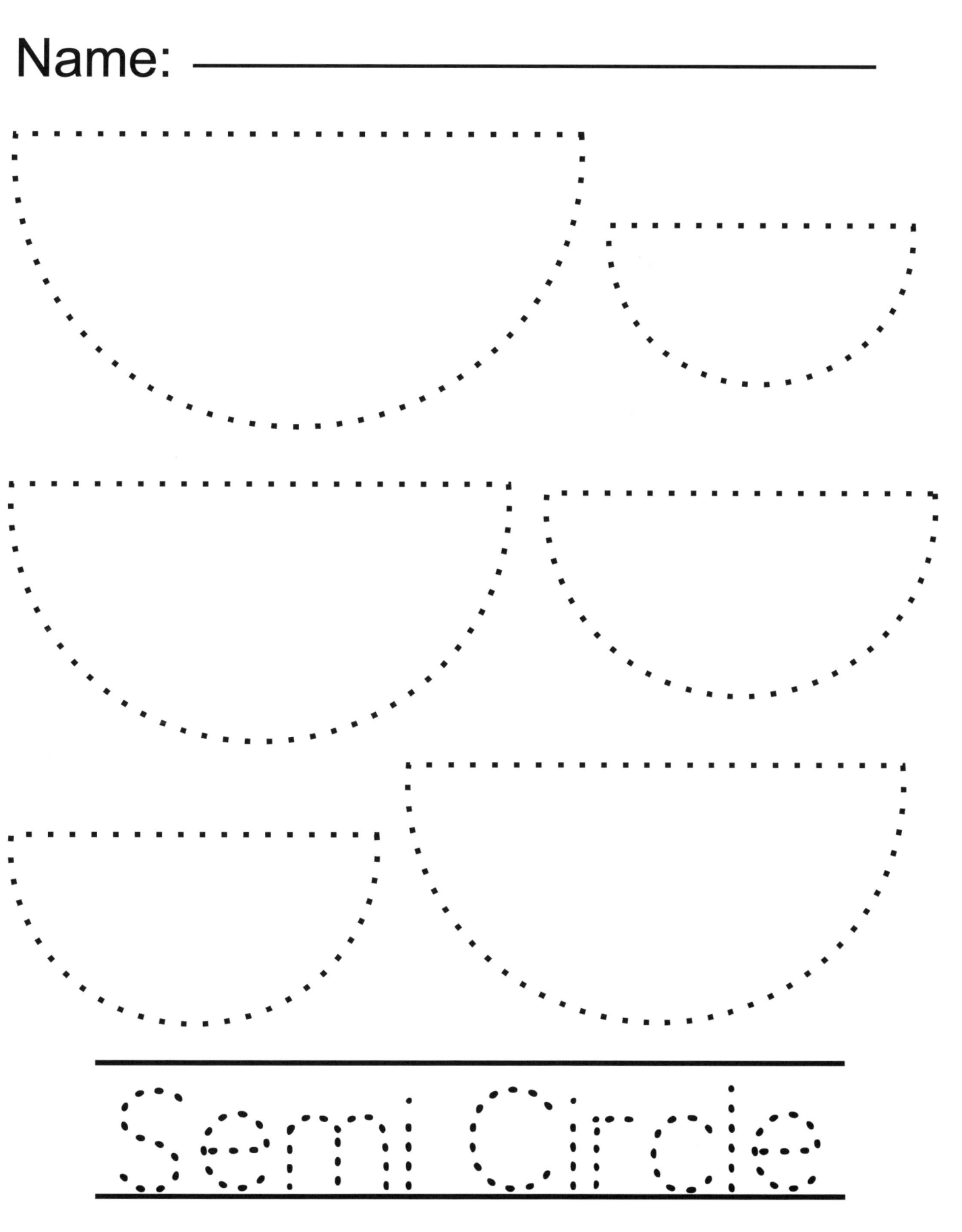

Semi Circle

Name: _____

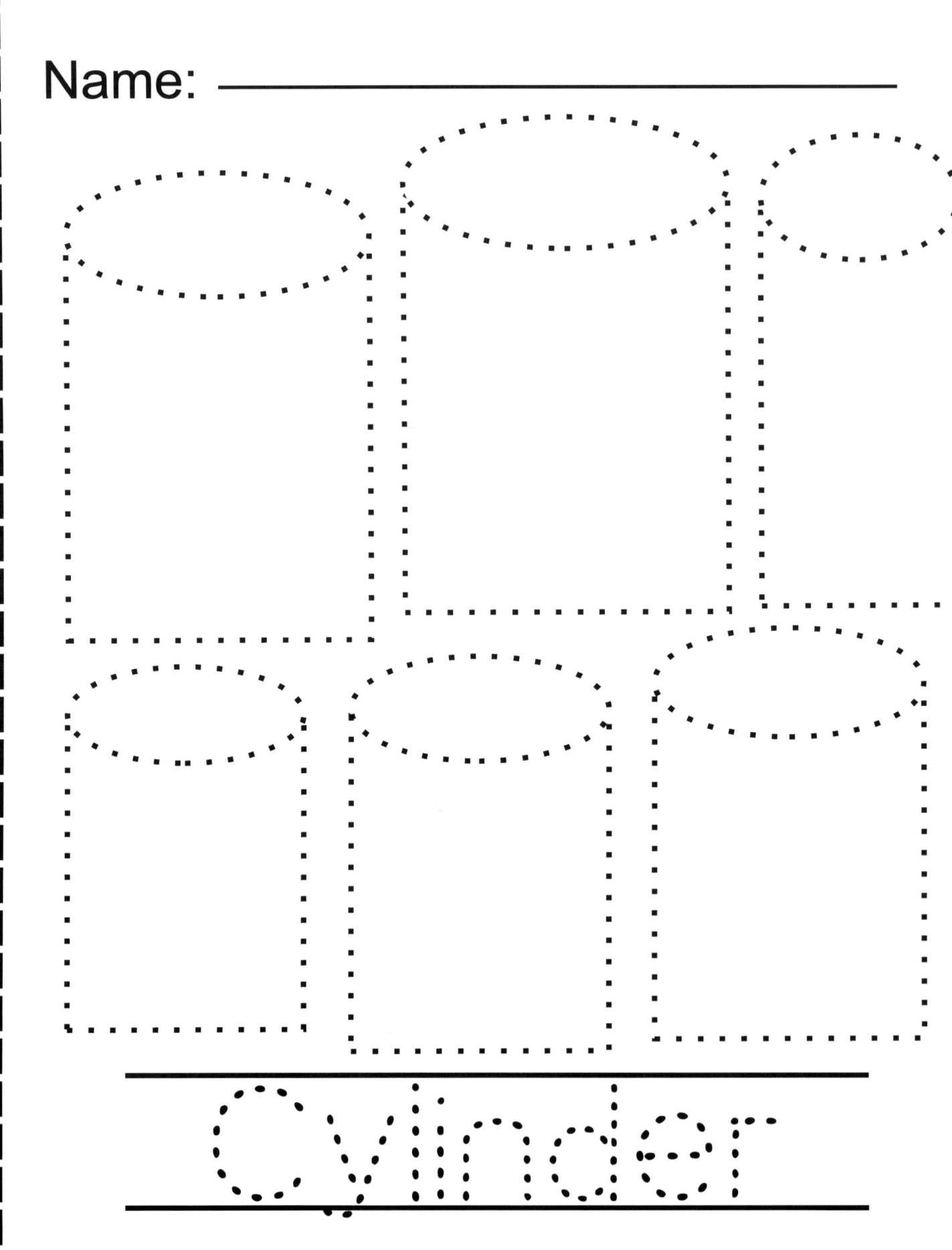

Cylinder

Name: _____

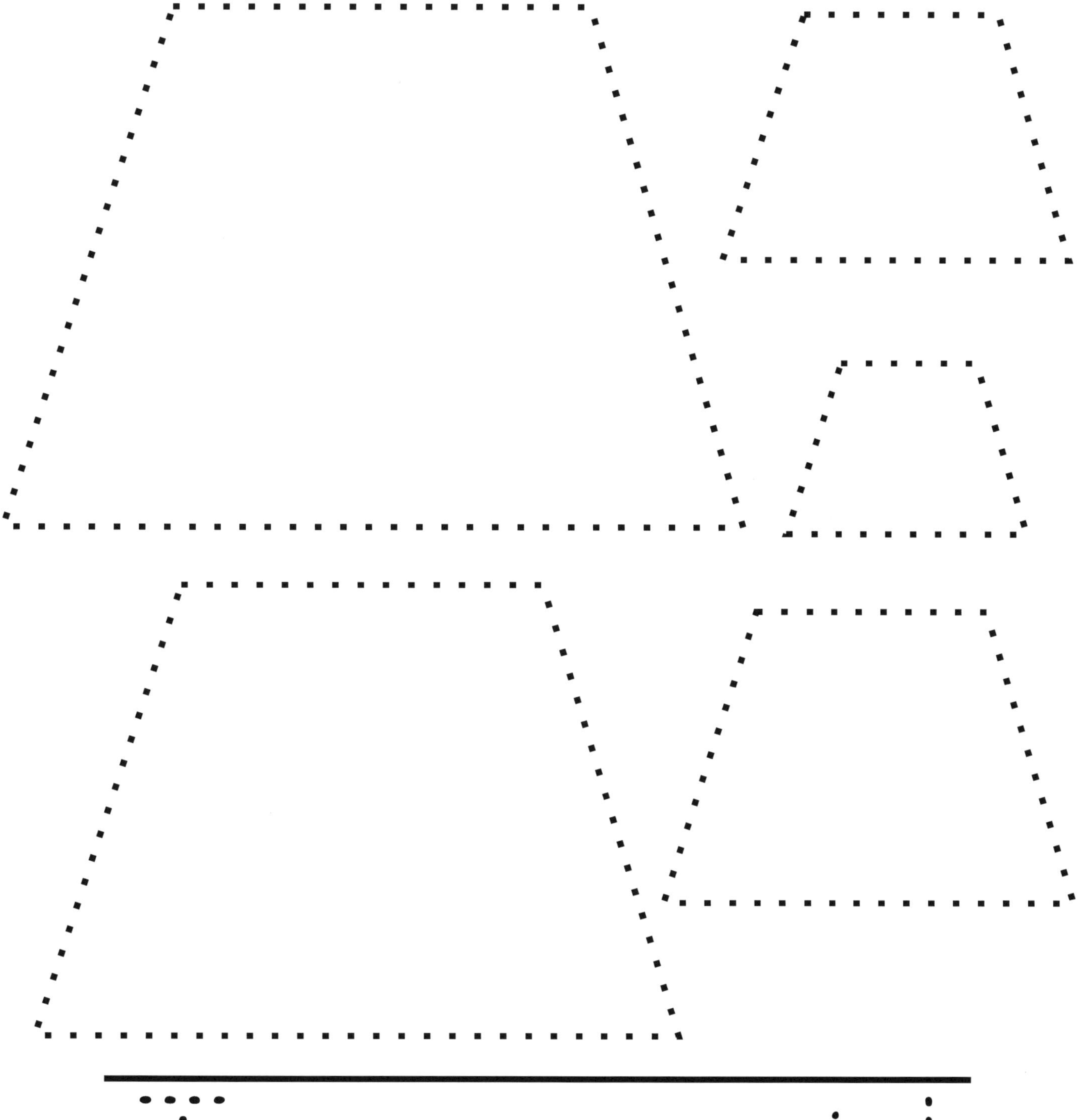

Trapezoid

Name: _____

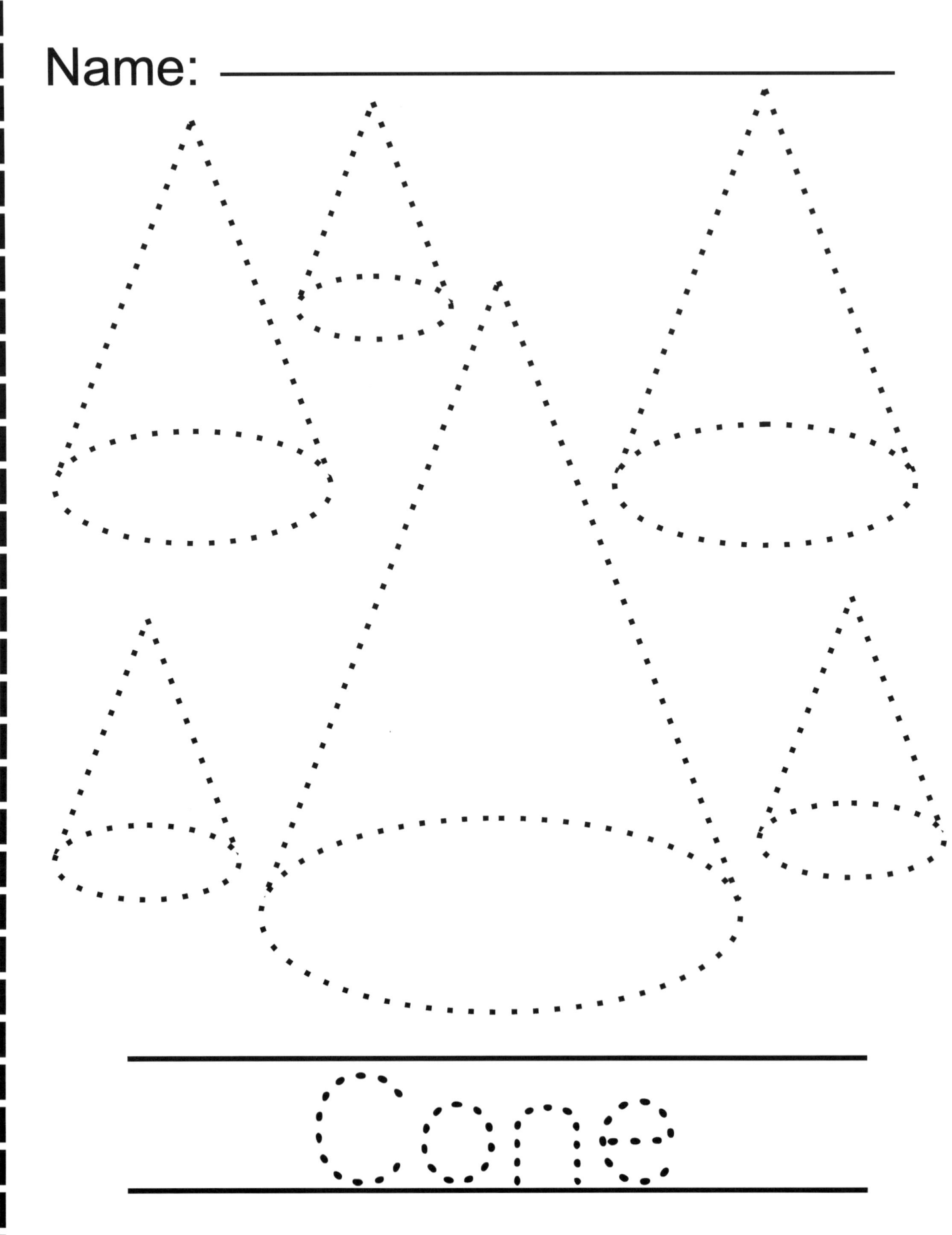

Name: _____

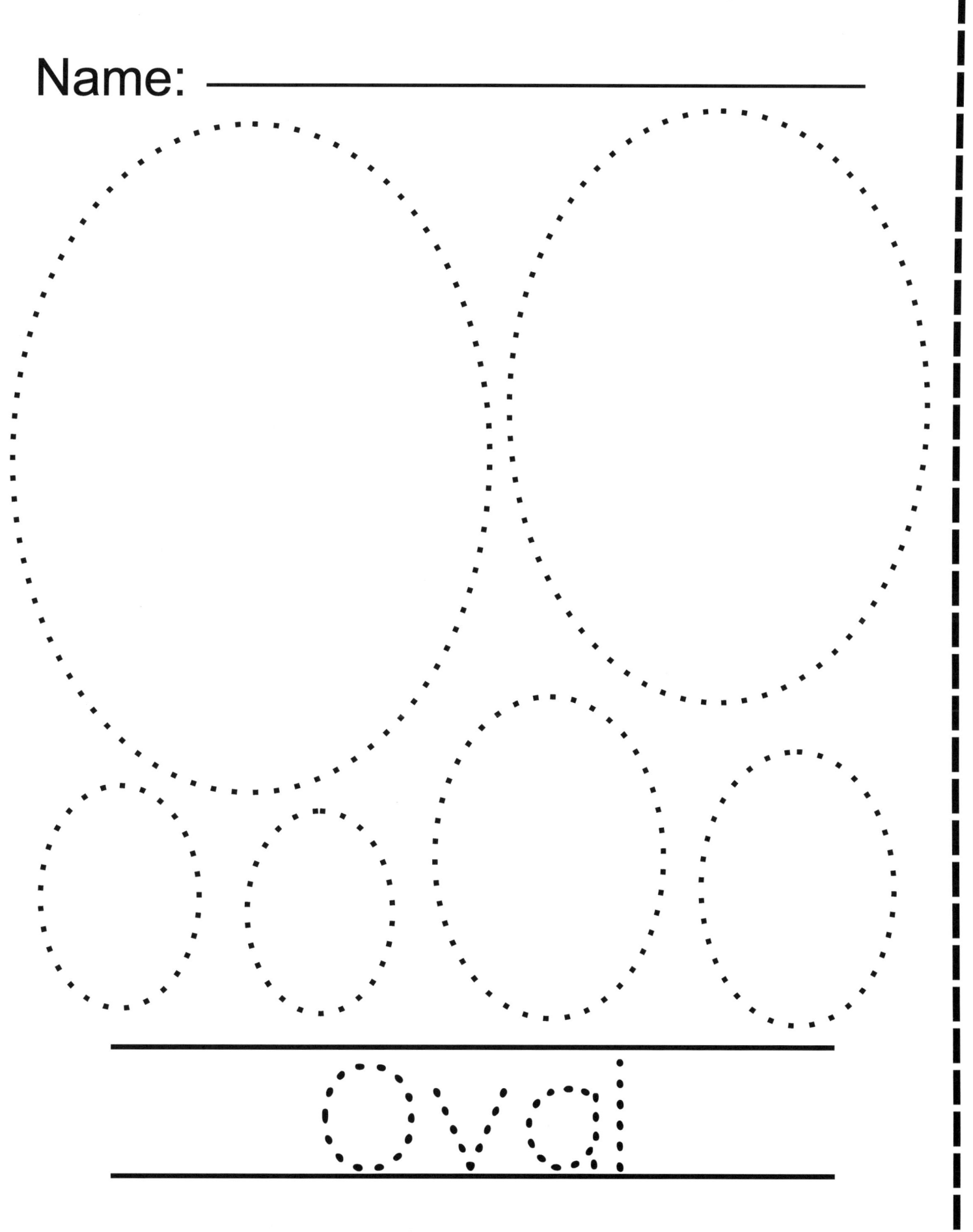

oval

Name: _____

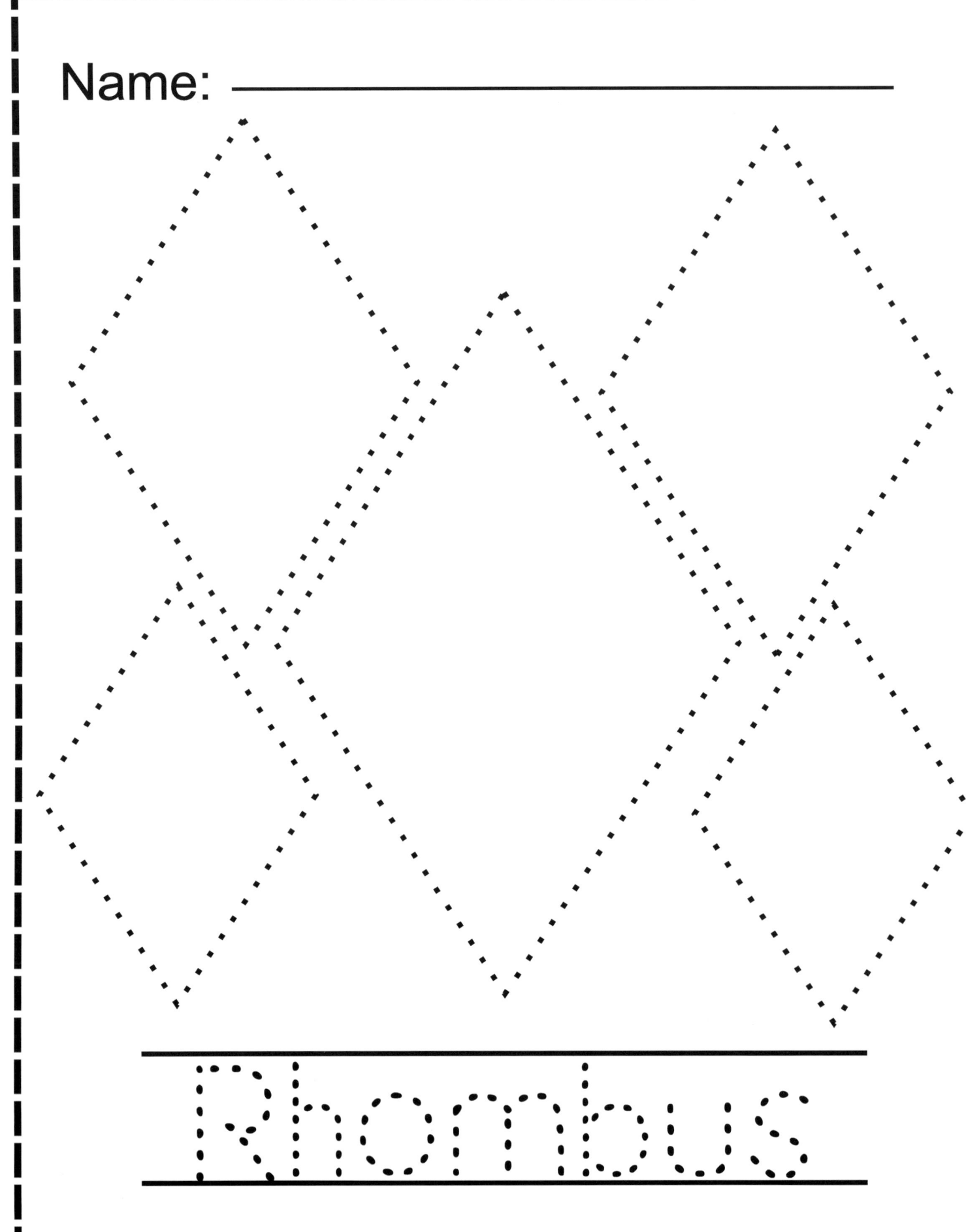

Name: _____

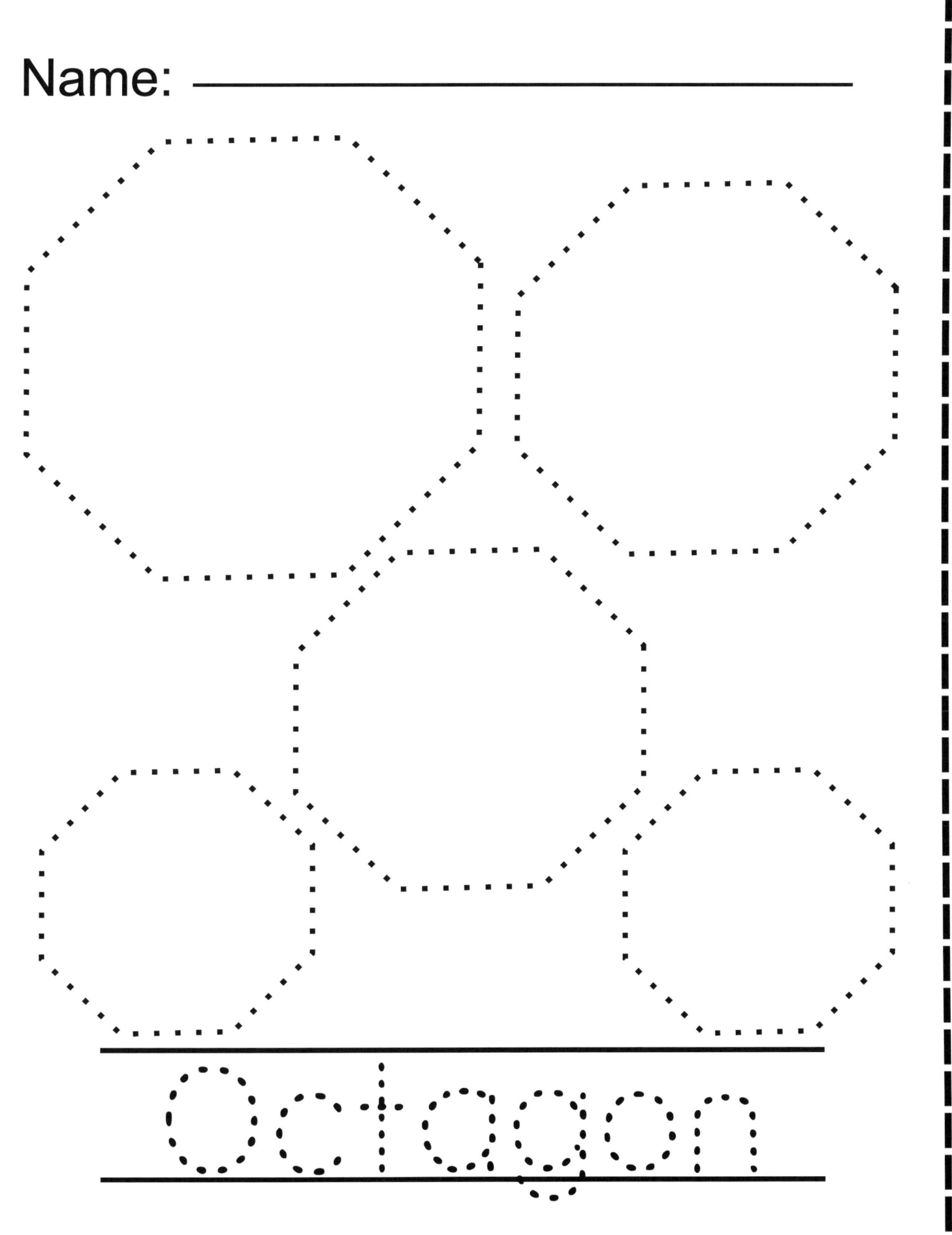

Name: _____

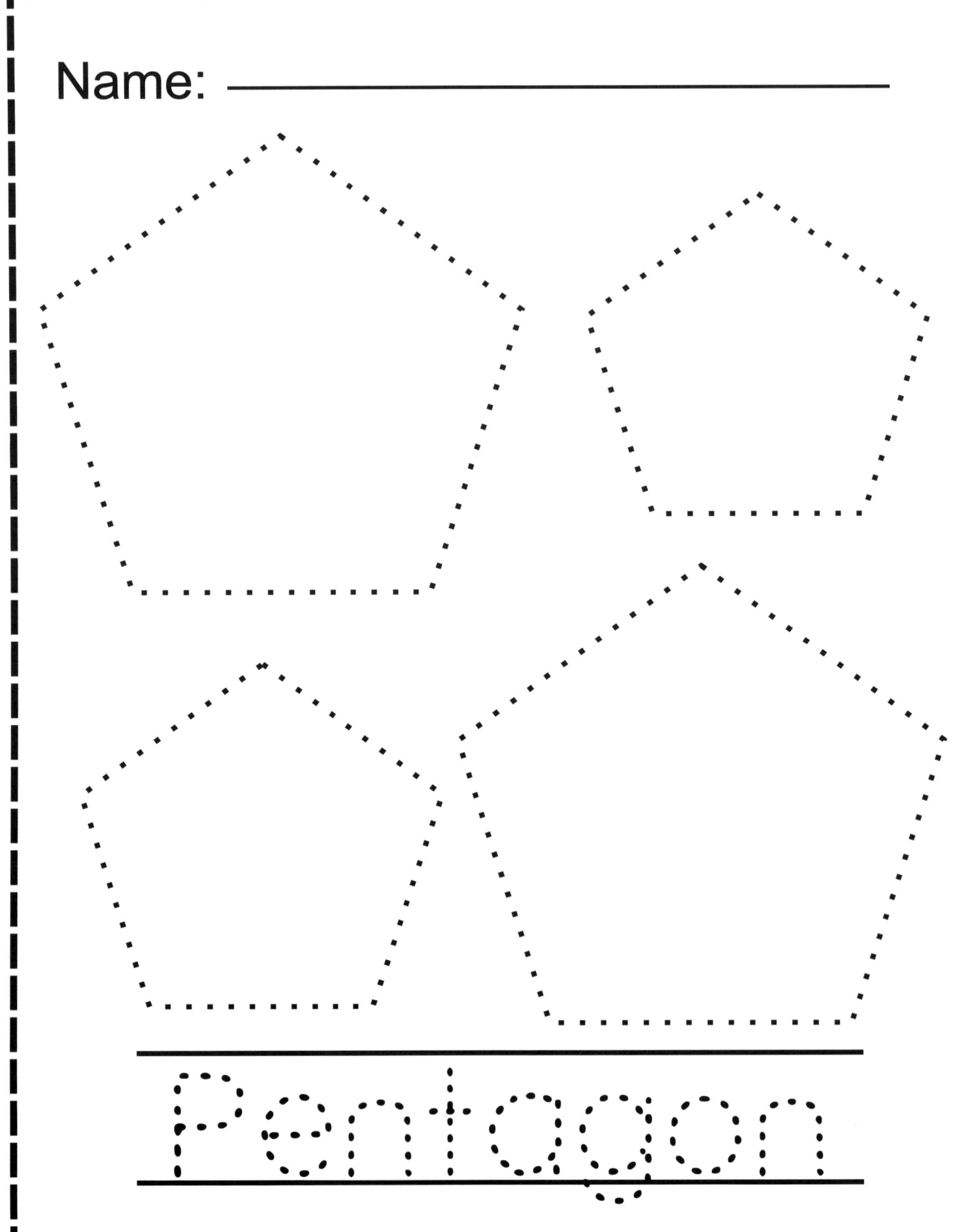

Pentagon

Name: _____

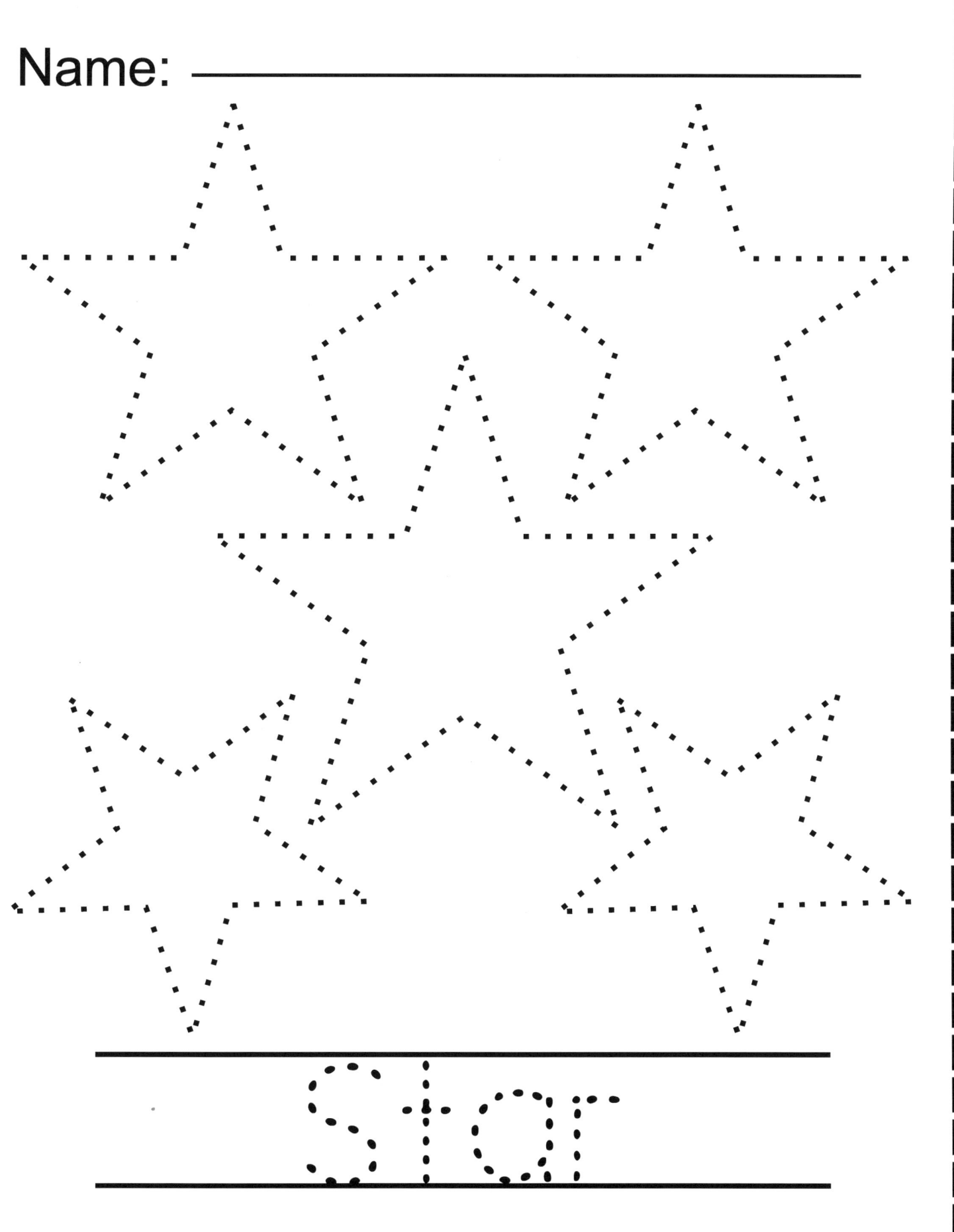

Number Tracing

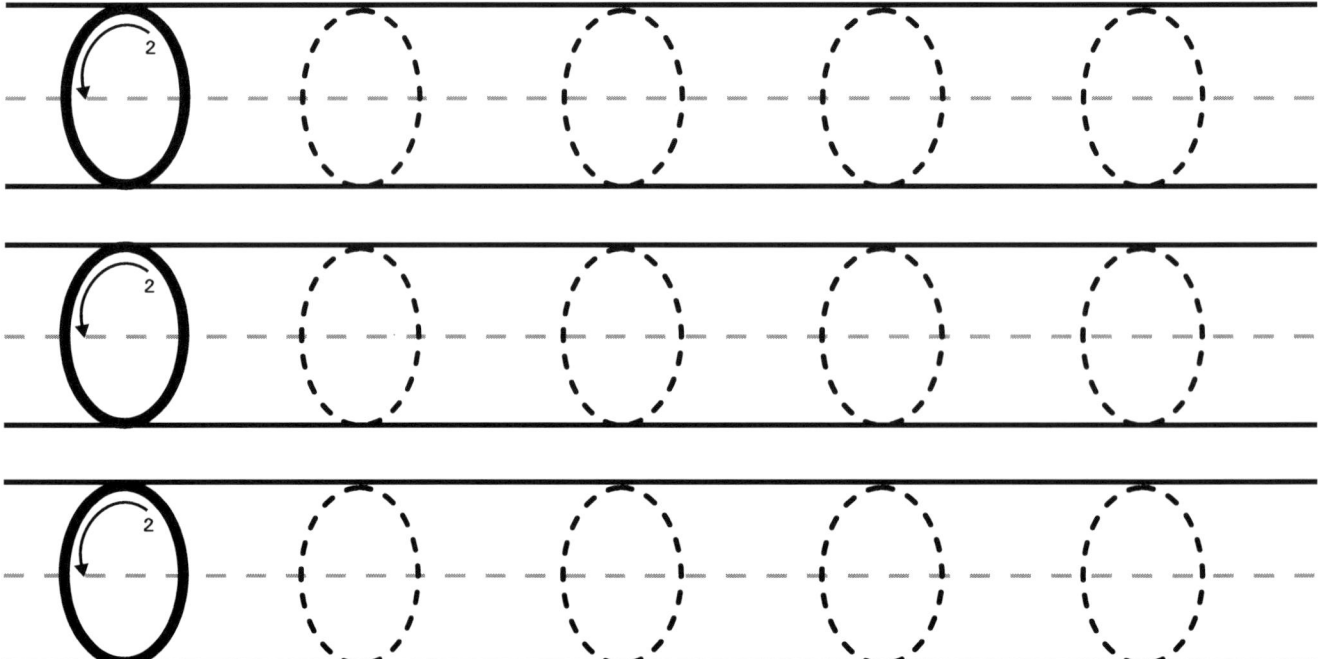

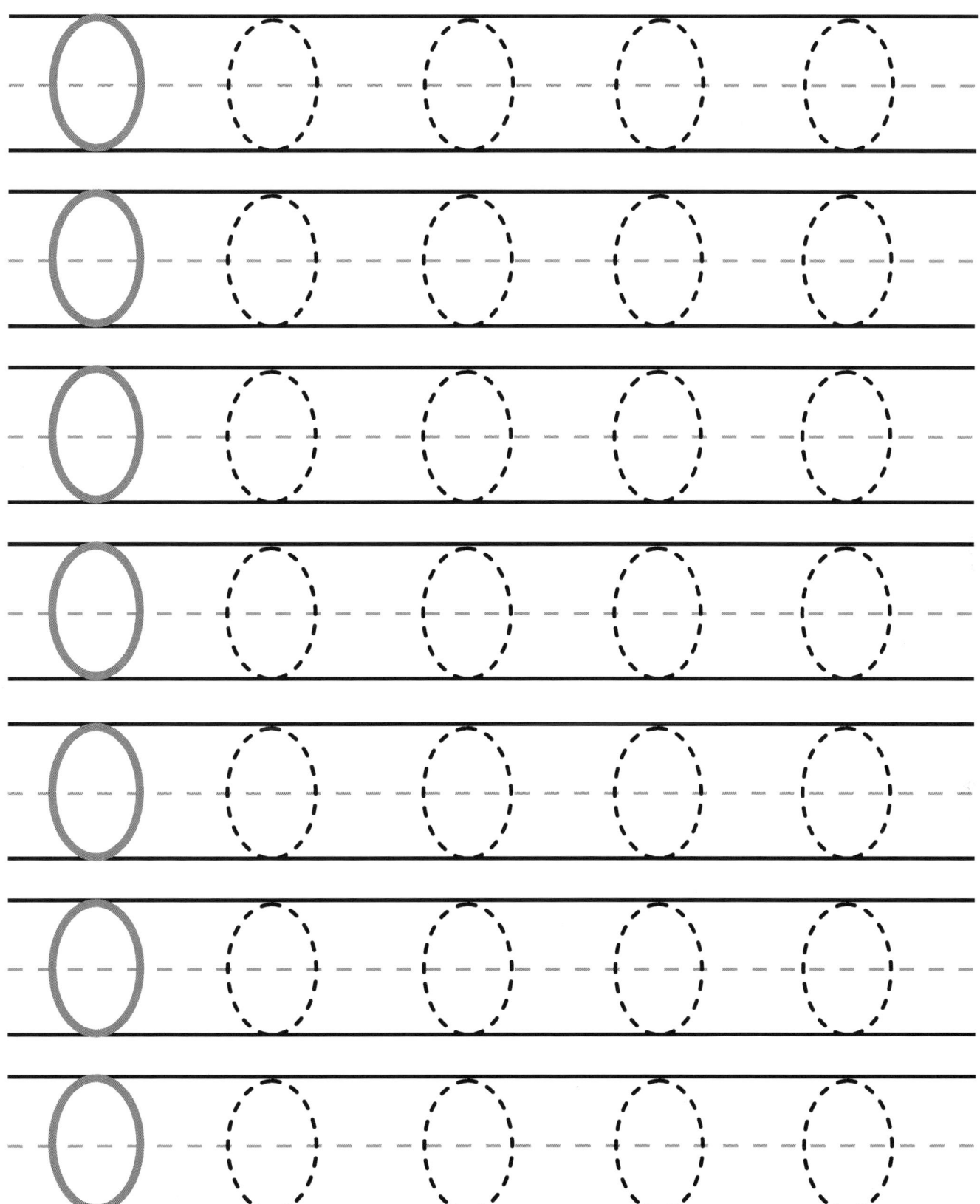

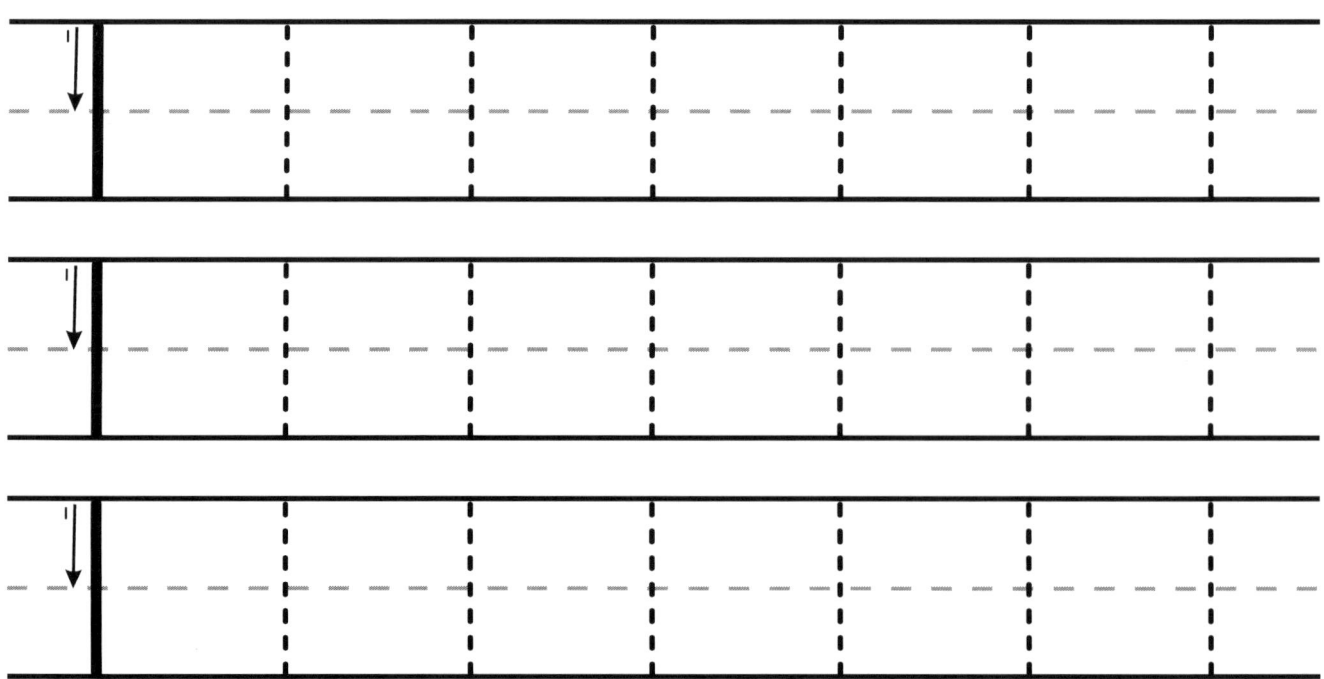

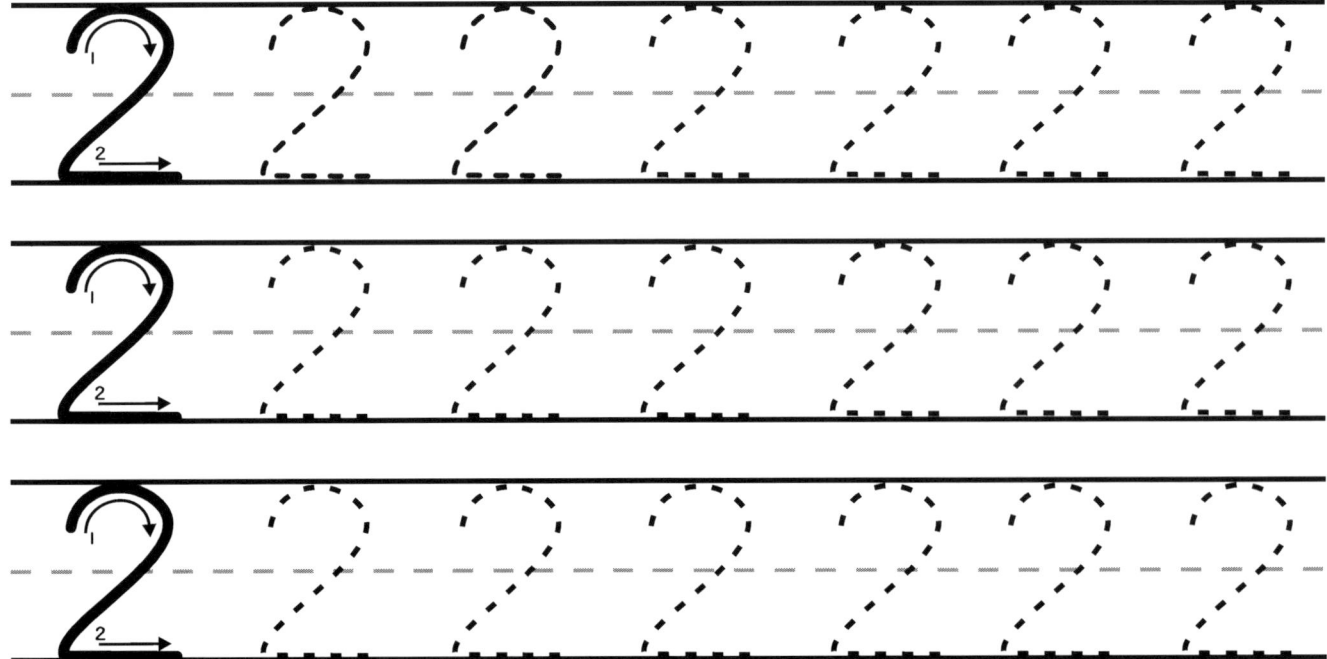

2 2 2 2 2 2 2

2 2 2 2 2 2 2

2 2 2 2 2 2 2

2 2 2 2 2 2 2

2 2 2 2 2 2 2

2 2 2 2 2 2 2

2 2 2 2 2 2 2

3
Three

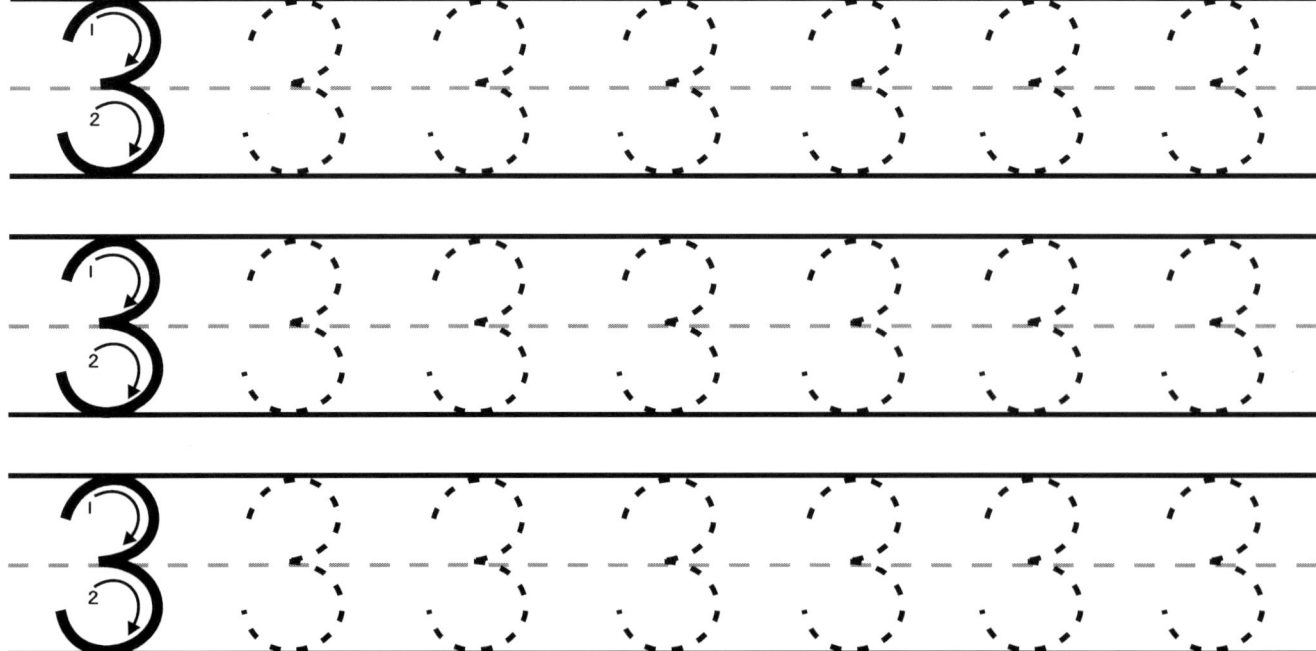

3 3 3 3 3 3 3

3 3 3 3 3 3 3

3 3 3 3 3 3 3

3 3 3 3 3 3 3

3 3 3 3 3 3 3

3 3 3 3 3 3 3

3 3 3 3 3 3 3

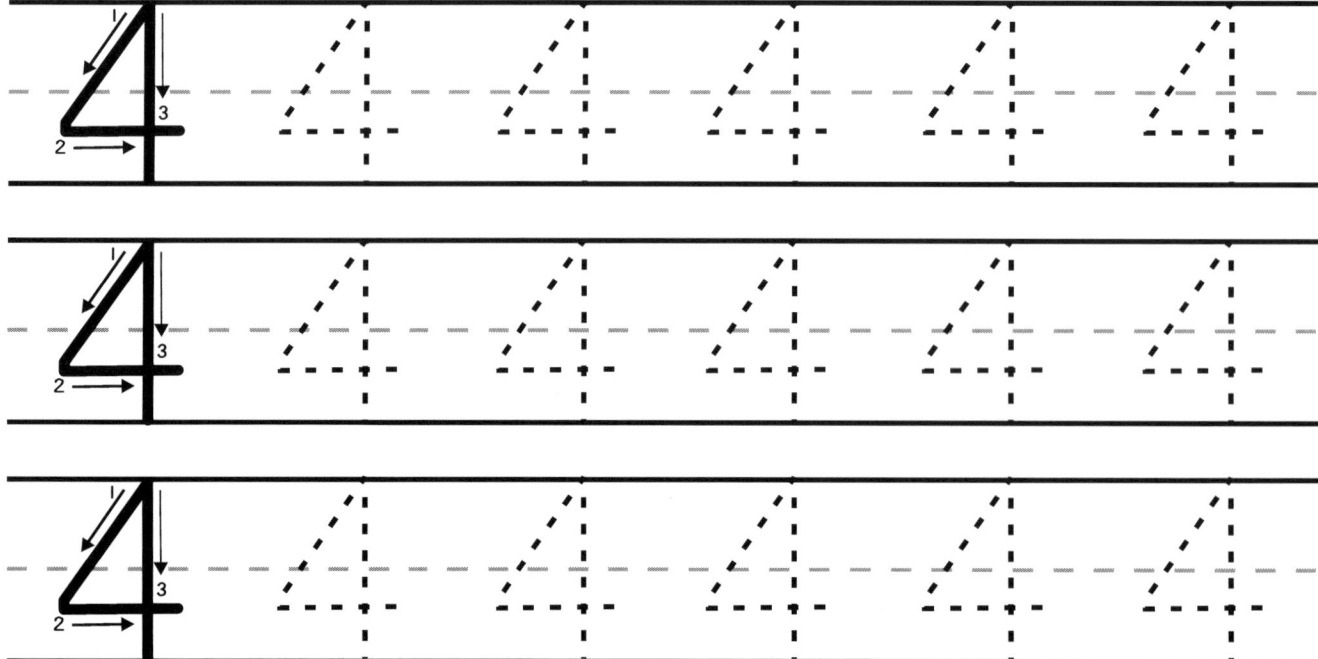

5 Five

5 5 5 5 5 5
5 5 5 5 5 5
5 5 5 5 5 5
5 5 5 5 5 5
5 5 5 5 5 5
5 5 5 5 5 5
5 5 5 5 5 5

6
Six

6 6 6 6 6 6
6 6 6 6 6 6
6 6 6 6 6 6
6 6 6 6 6 6
6 6 6 6 6 6
6 6 6 6 6 6
6 6 6 6 6 6

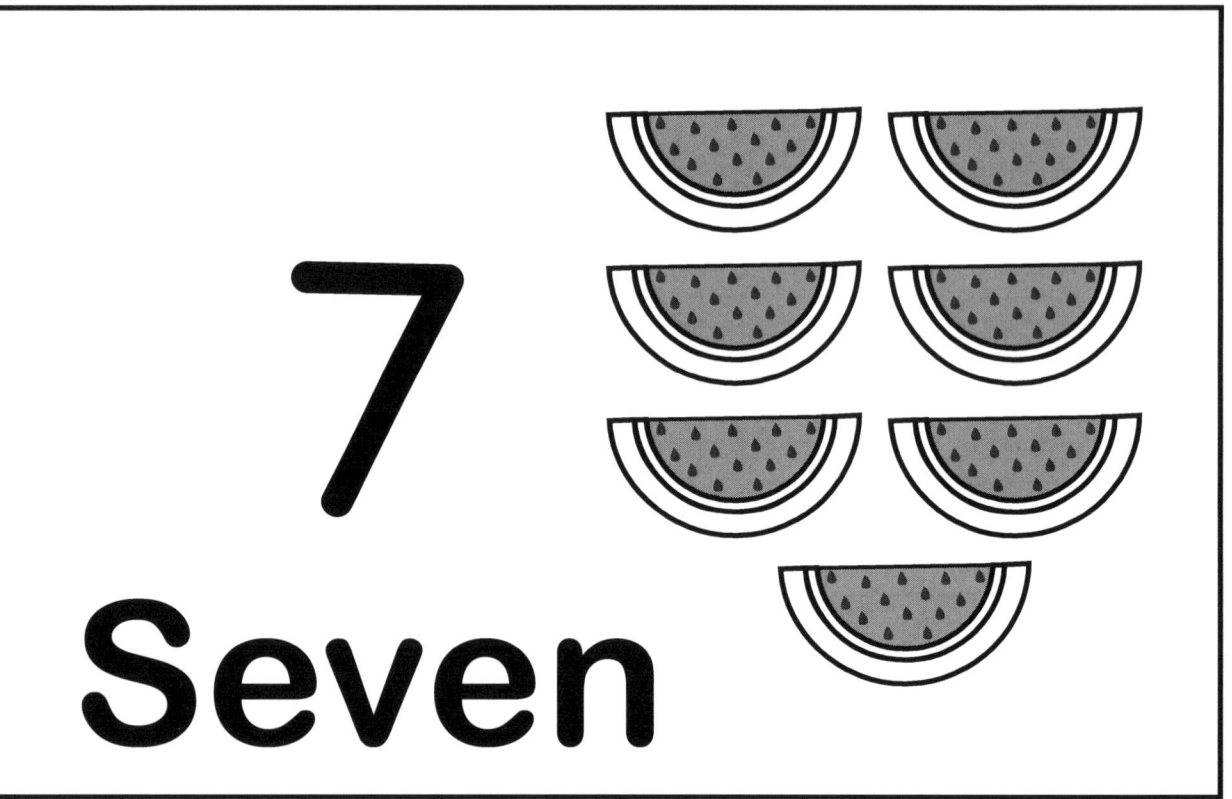

7
Seven

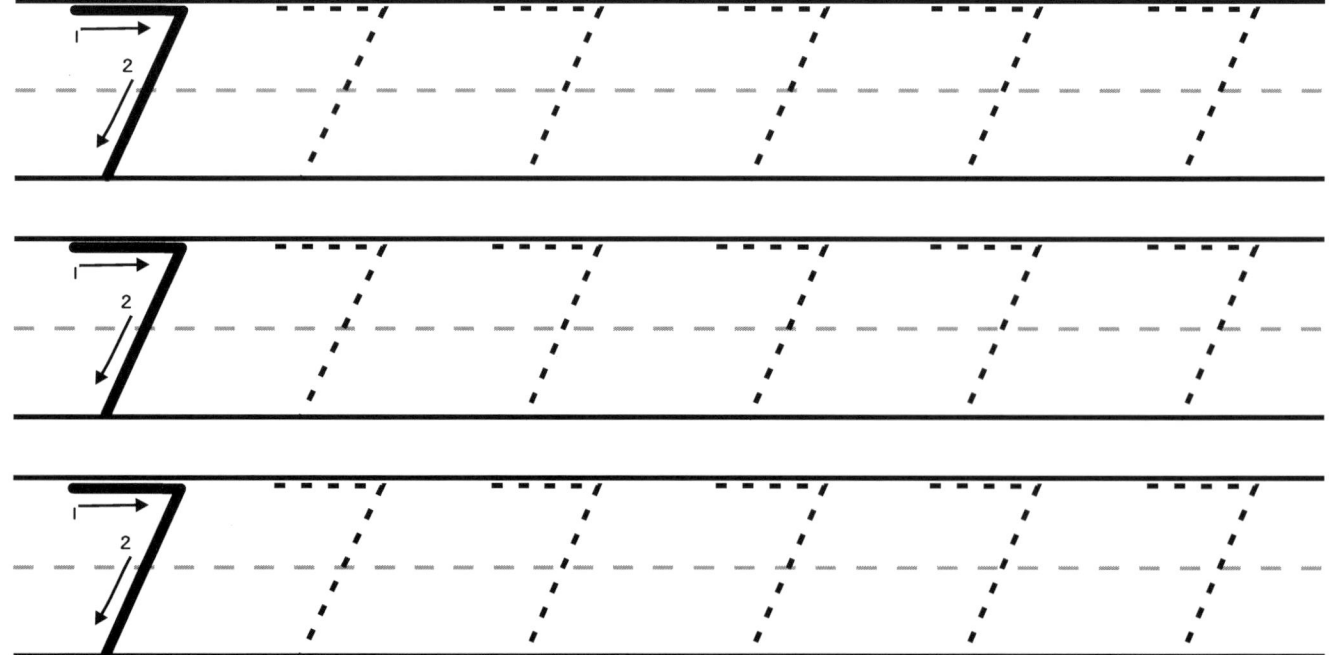

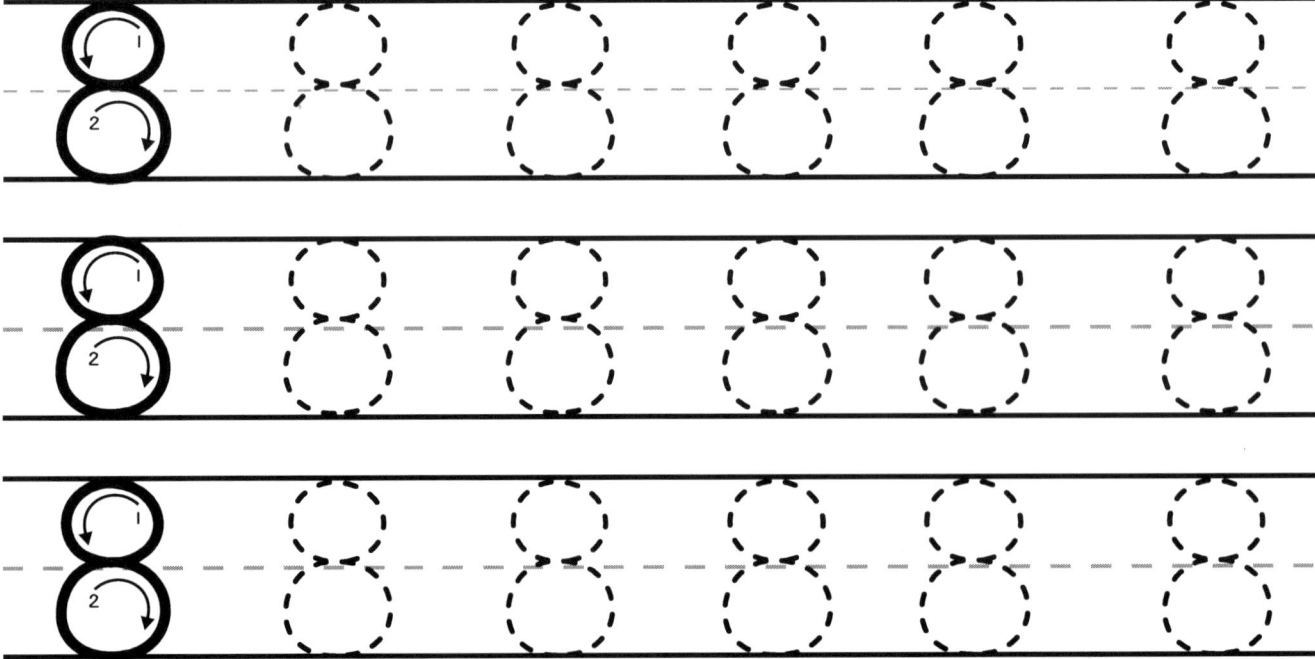

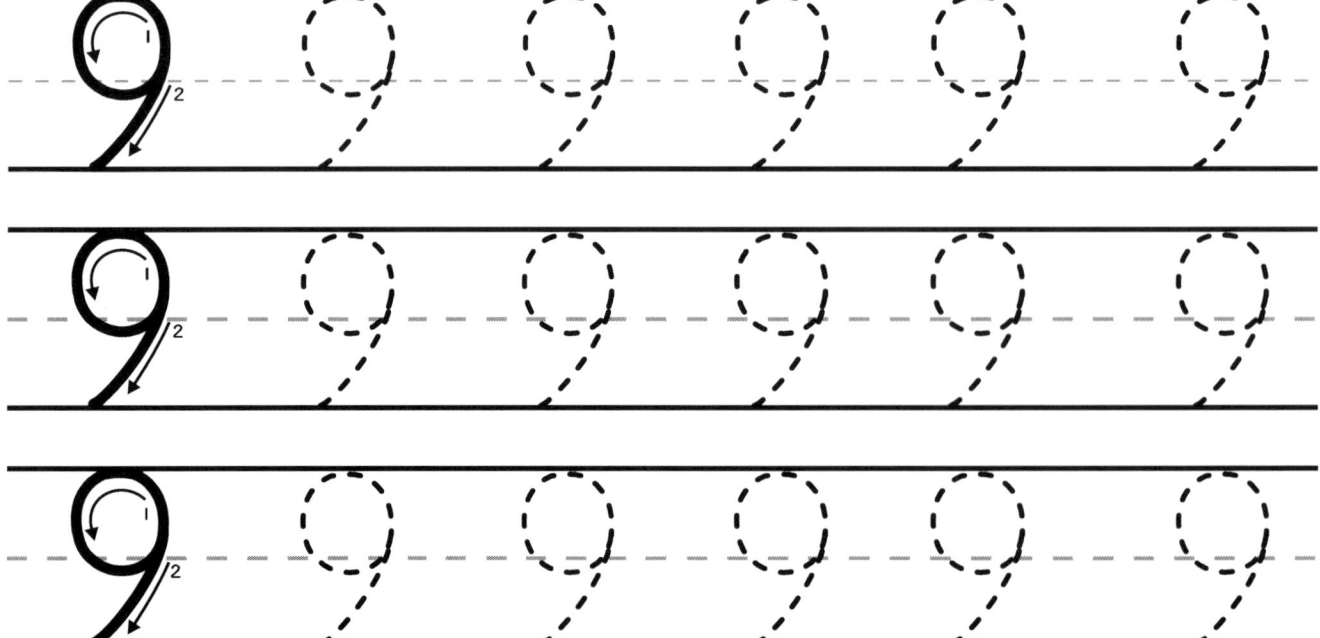

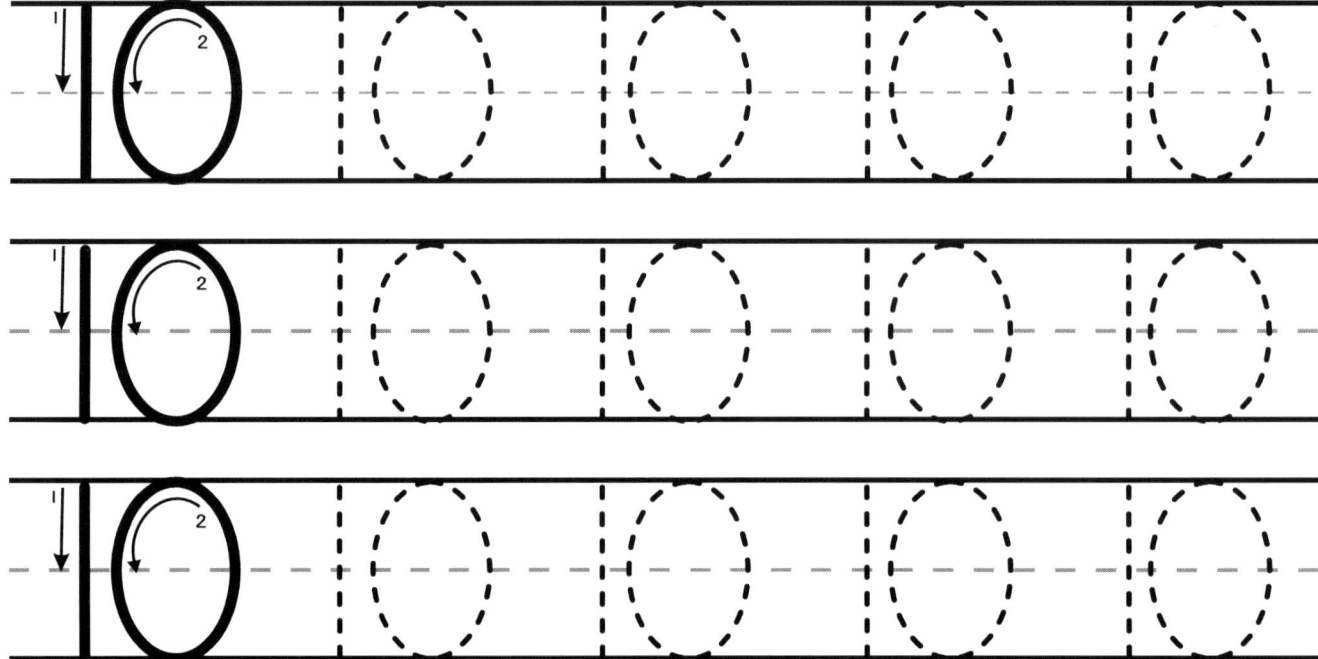

Counting fruit

How many pieces of fruit do you see? Circle the number.

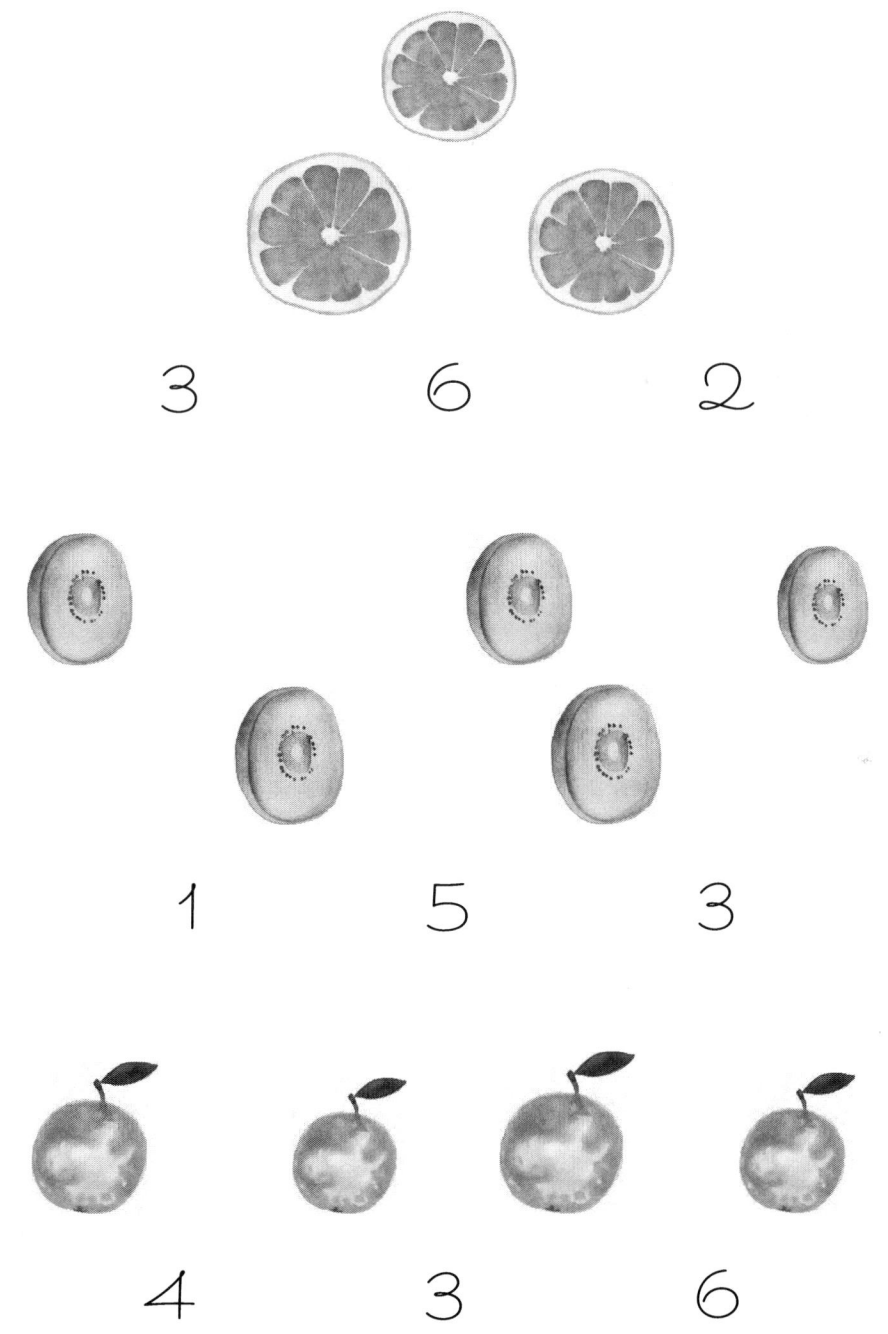

Counting fruit

How many pieces of fruit do you see? Circle the number.

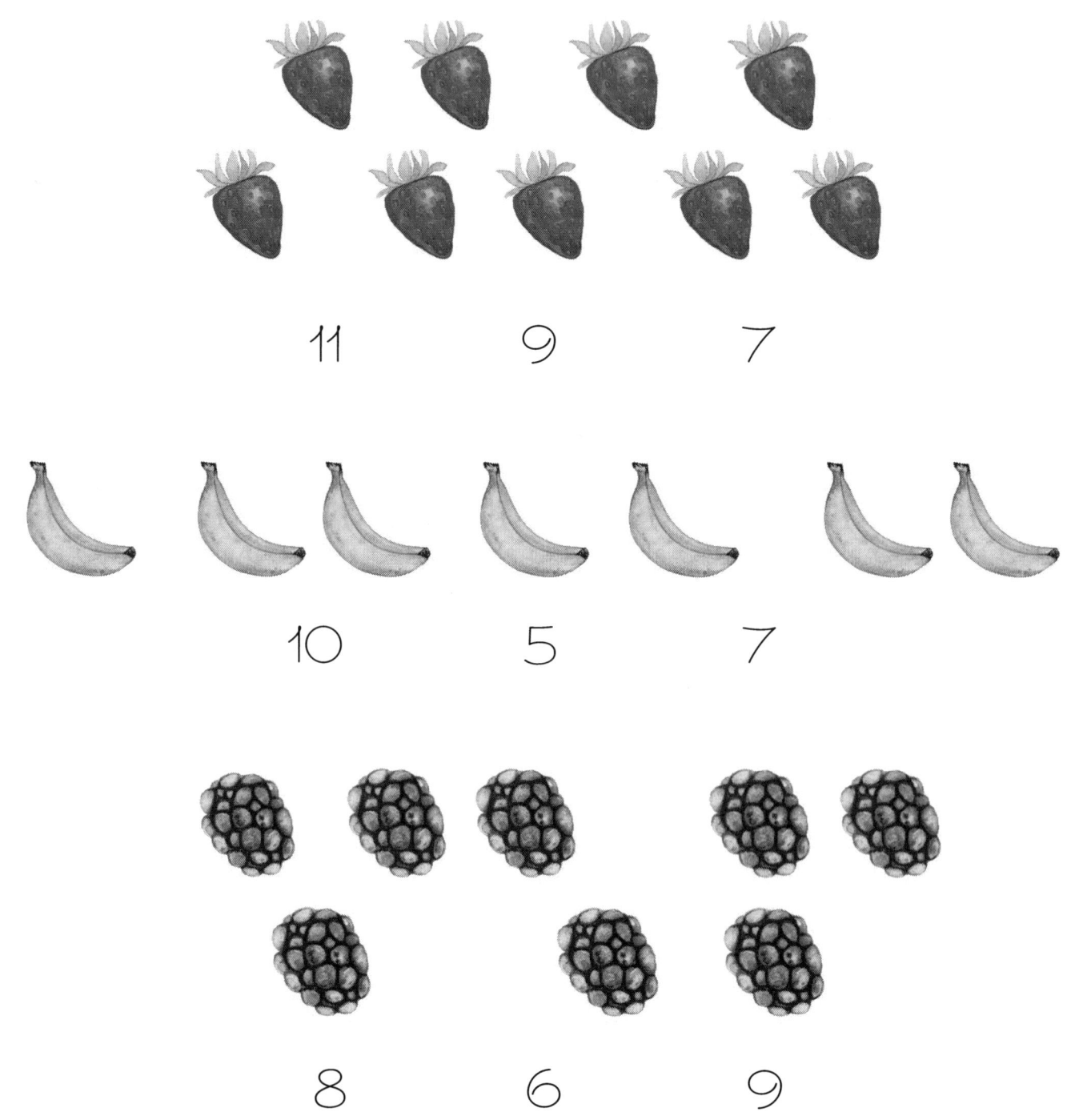

Missing numbers

Which numbers are missing? Fill them in.

1	2		4	5
6		8		10

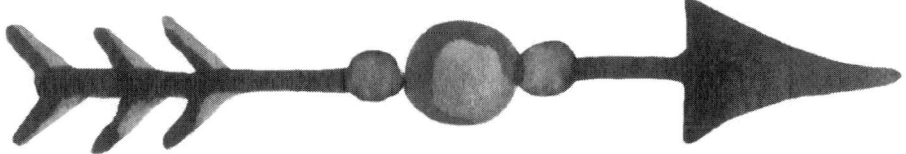

11		13	14	
	17		19	20

Missing numbers

Which numbers are missing? Fill them in.

1		3	4	
	7		9	10

11	12			15
16		18		20

Missing numbers

Which numbers are missing? Fill them in.

10	11		13	14
15		17		19

20		22	23	
	26		28	29

designstudioteti.etsy.com

Count and match

Count the items and match them with a number on the right.

Count and match

Count the items and match them with a number on the right.

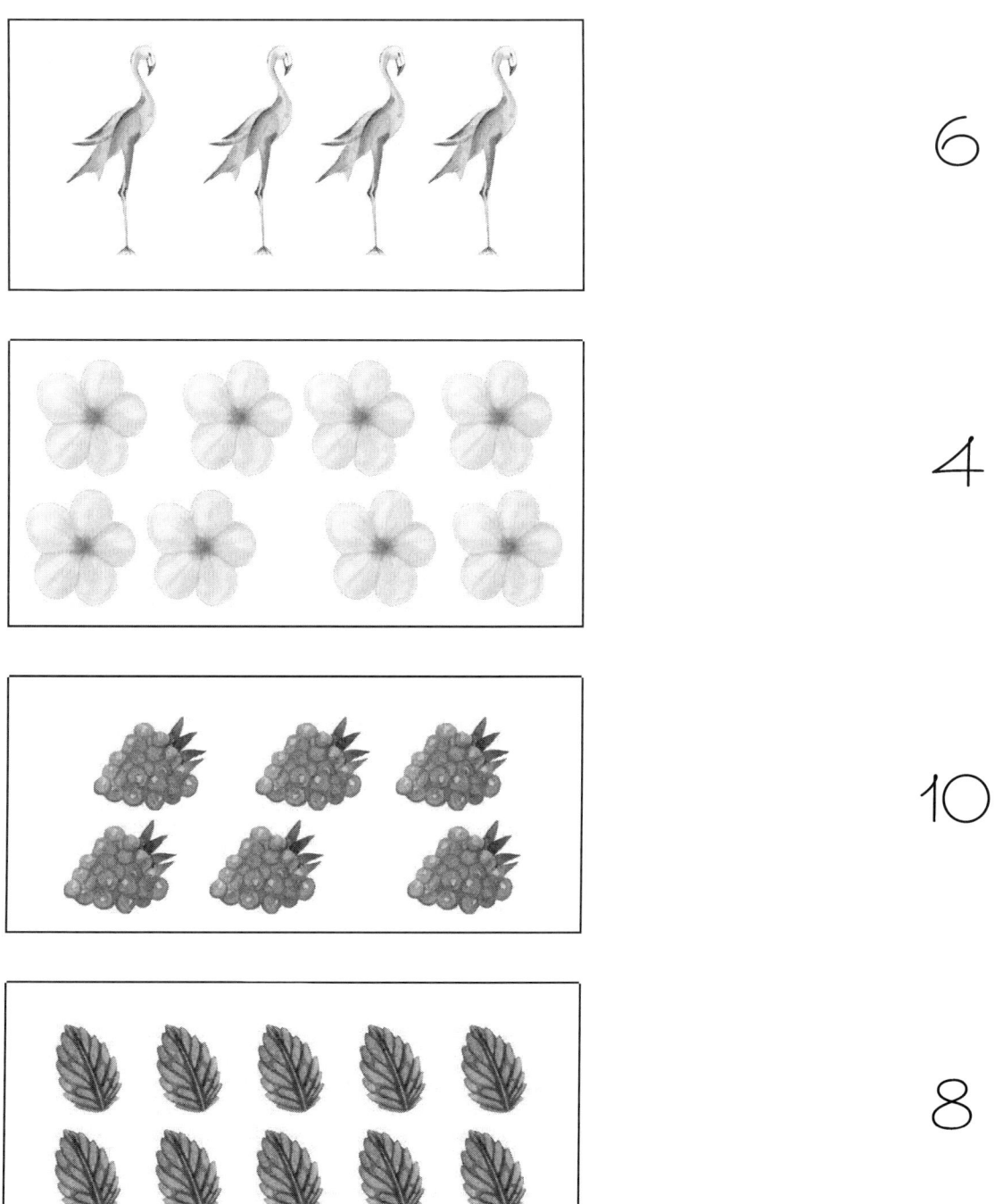

Picture addition

Add the pictures.

2 + 1 = ____   2 + 2 = ____

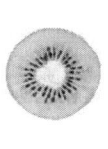 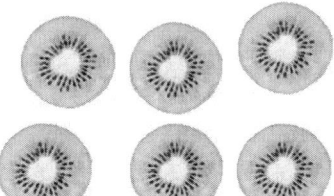   

1 + 6 = ____   4 + 3 = ____

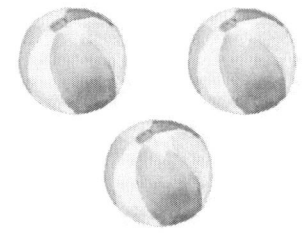    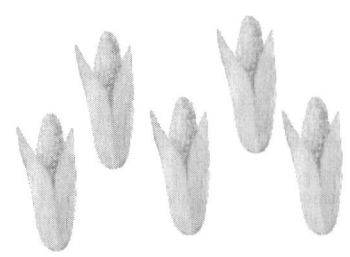

3 + 2 = ____   5 + 2 = ____

Picture addition

Add the pictures.

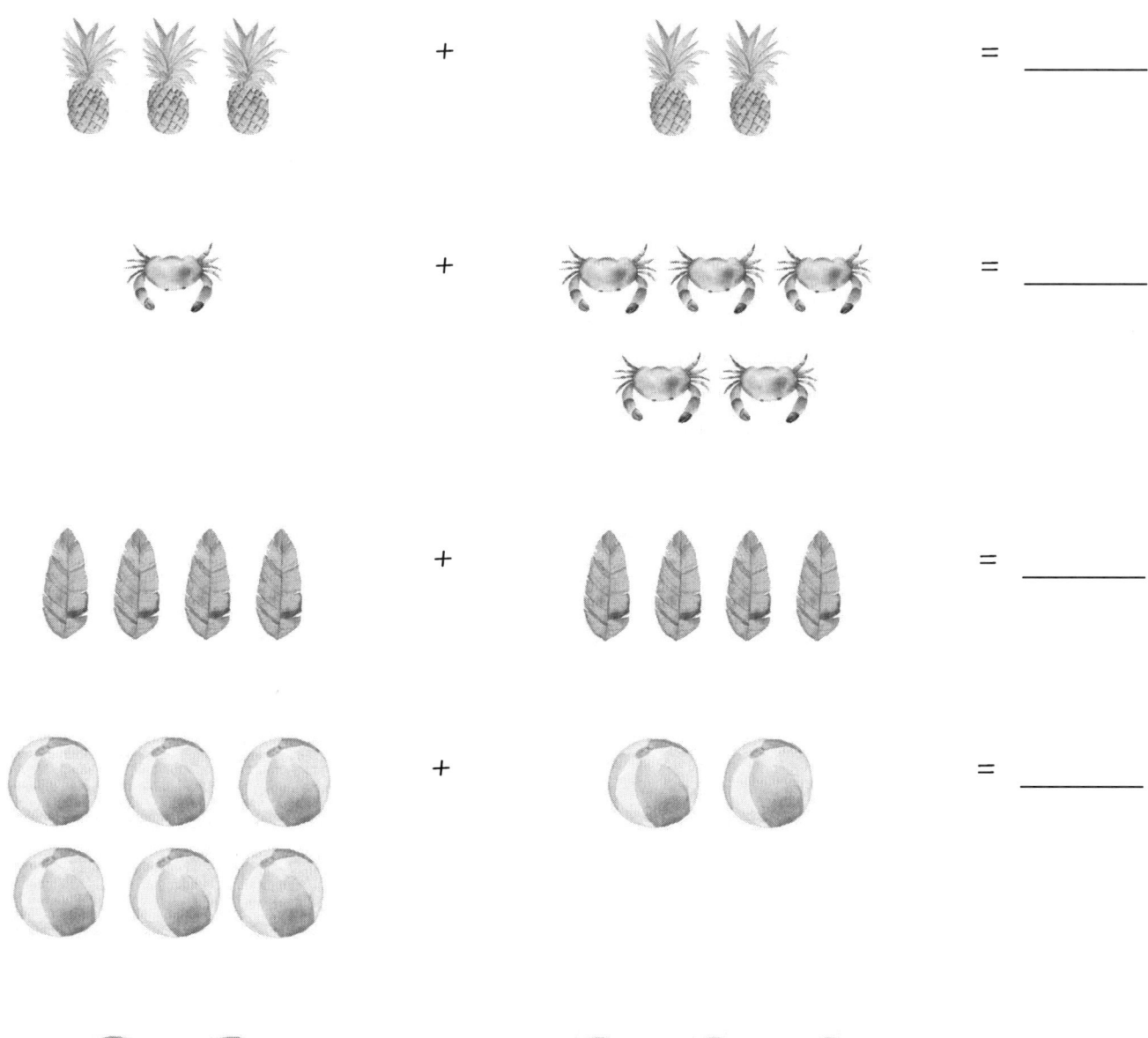

Picture addition

How many pieces of fruit are missing?

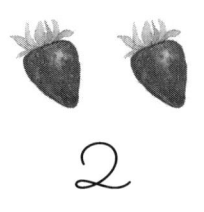 + 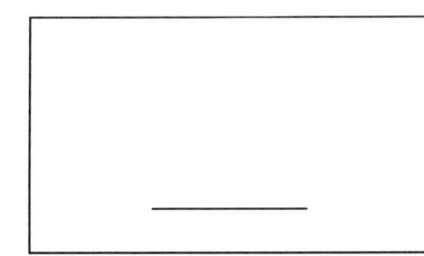 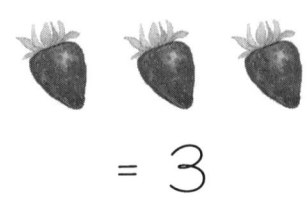 = 3

2

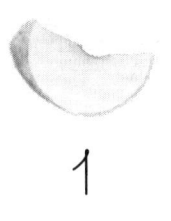 + 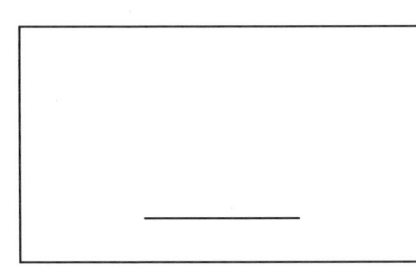 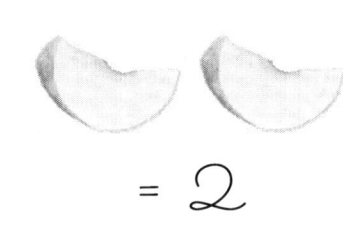 = 2

1

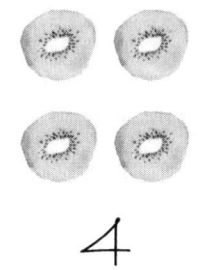 + 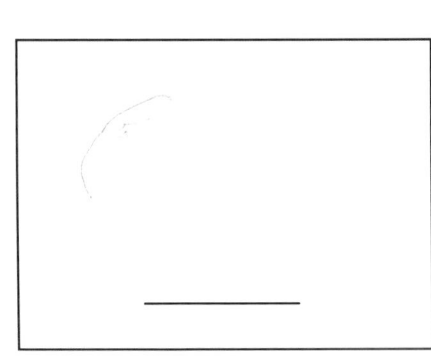 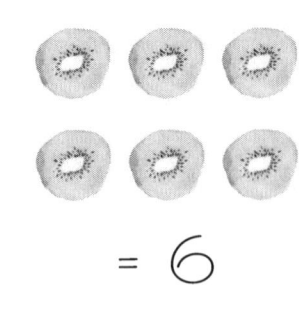 = 6

4

 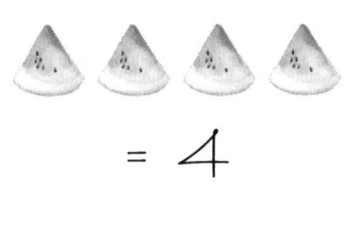 = 4

1

designstudioteti.etsy.com

Picture subtraction

How many pictures remain?

   3 - 1 = ___

   4 - 2 = ___

   5 - 1 = ___

   3 - 2 = ___

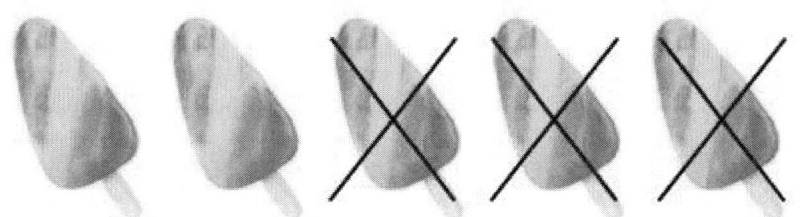   5 - 3 = ___

designstudioleti.etsy.com

Picture subtraction

How many pictures remain?

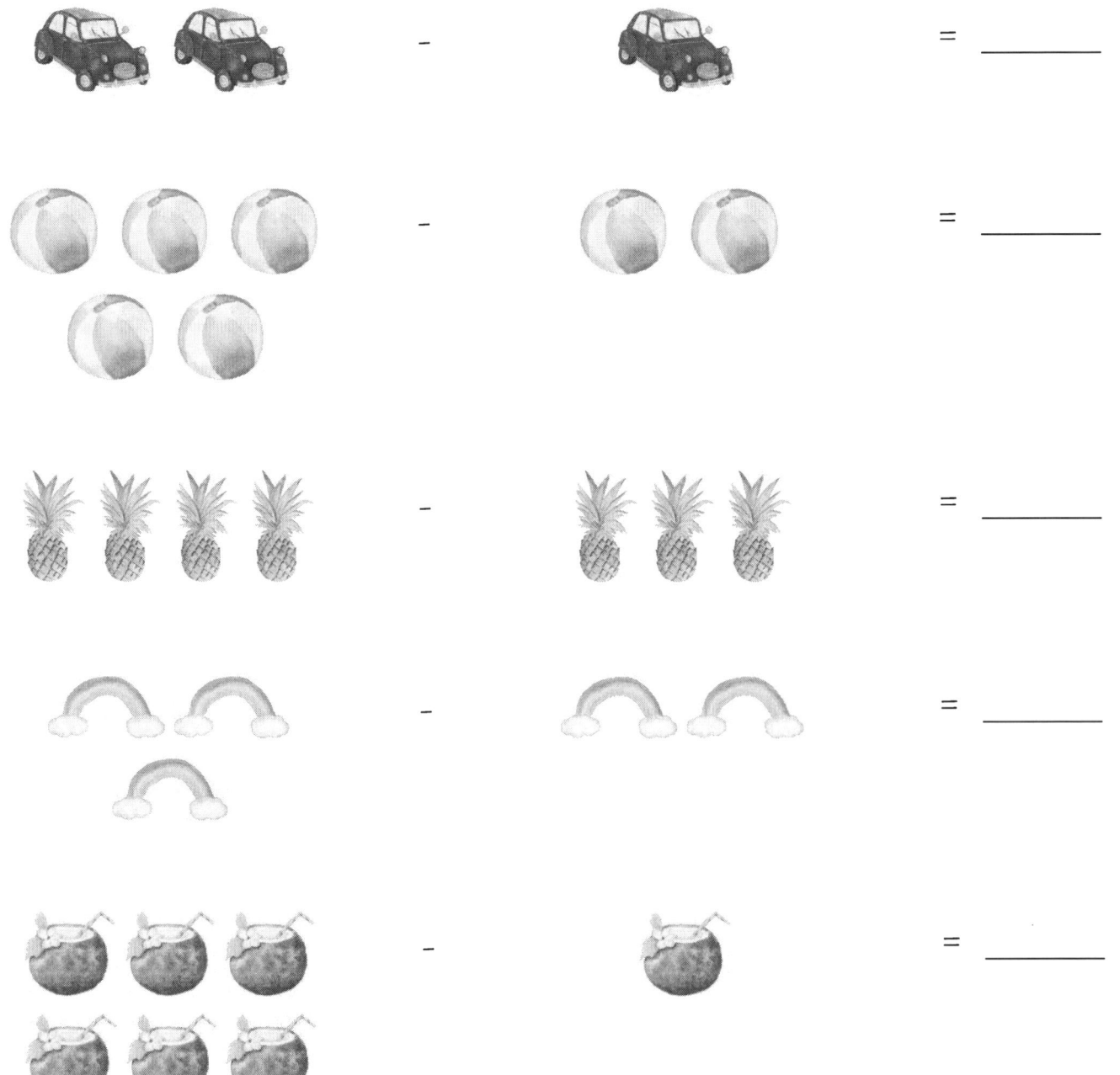

Picture subtraction

How many pieces are subtracted?

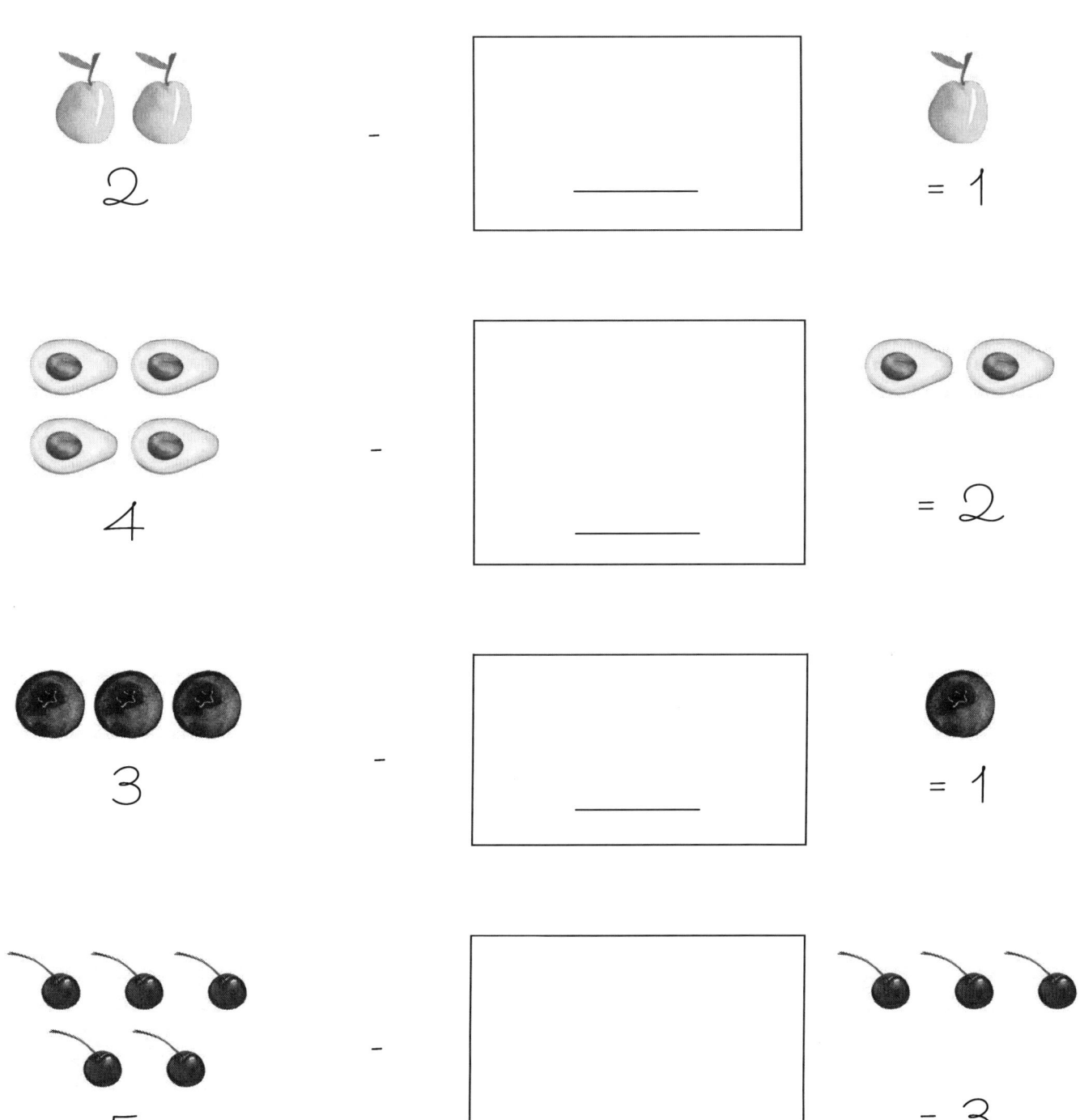

Least to greatest numbers

Arrange the numbers from least to greatest.

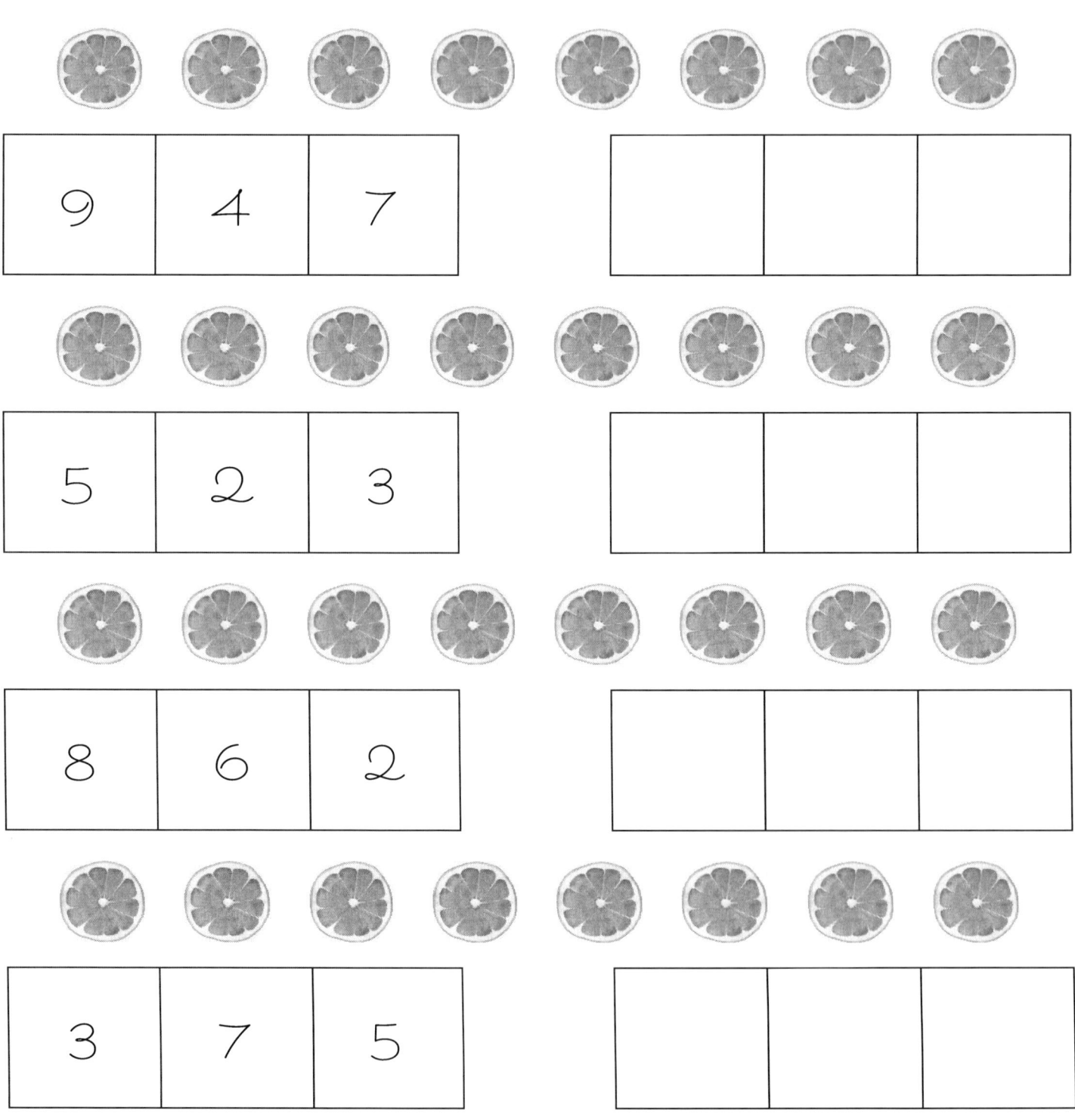

Least to greatest numbers

Arrange the numbers from least to greatest.

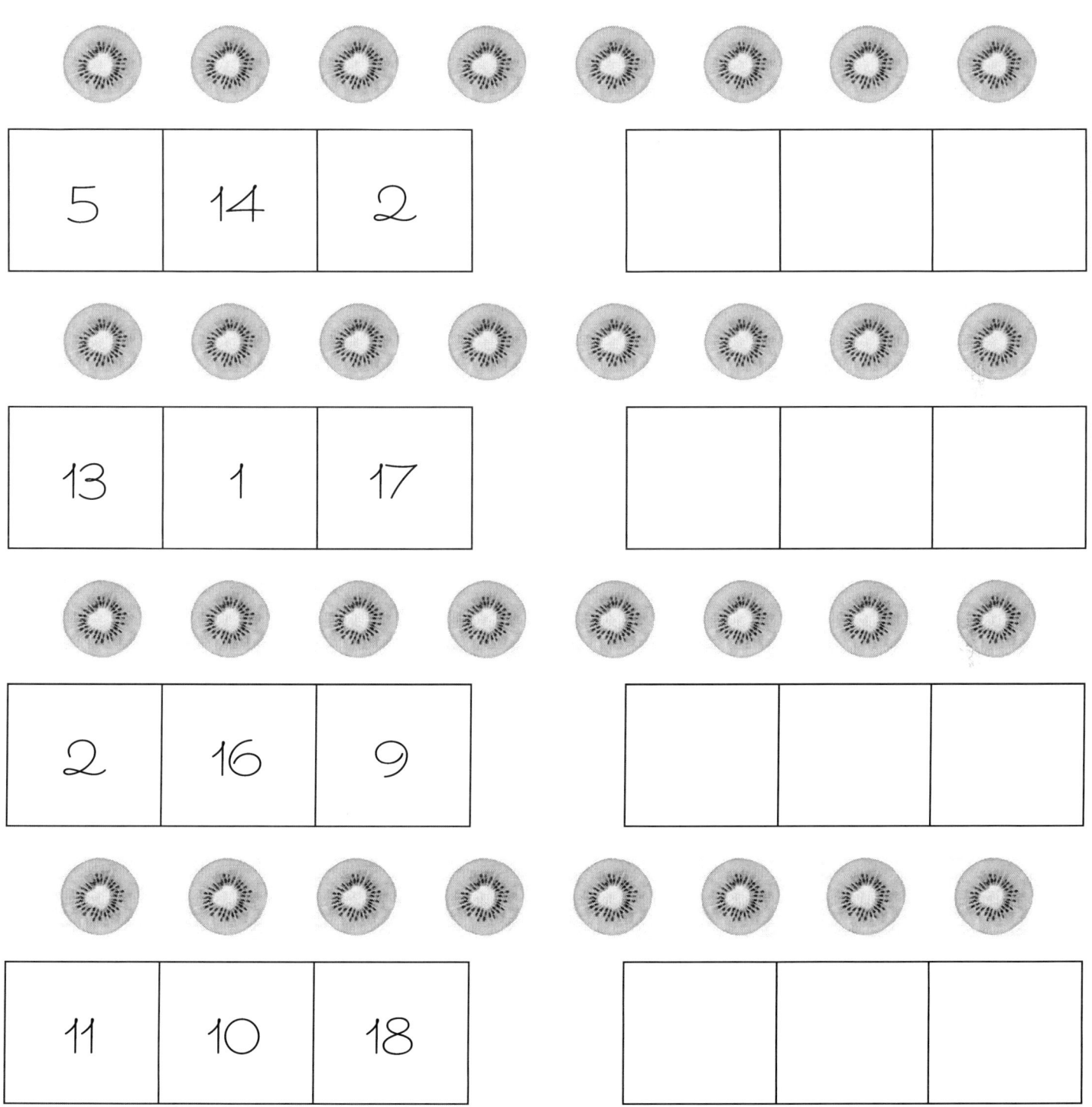

Let's make 10

Draw more to make 10. Finish the addition equation.

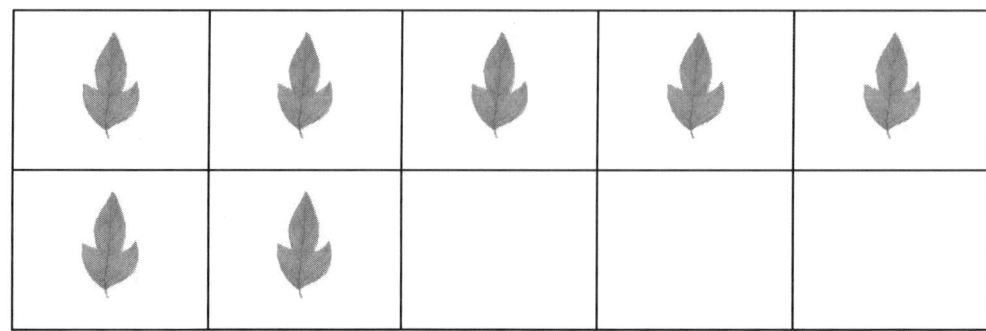

7 + ____ = 10

5 + ____ = 10

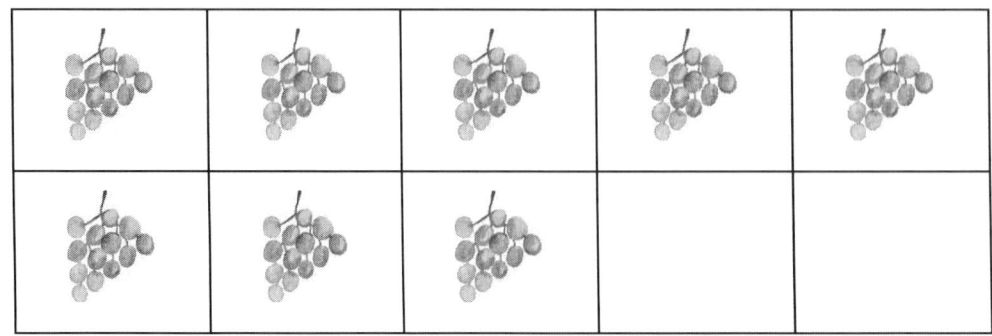

8 + ____ = 10

Let's make 10

Draw more to make 10. Finish the addition equation.

9 + ____ = 10

3 + ____ = 10

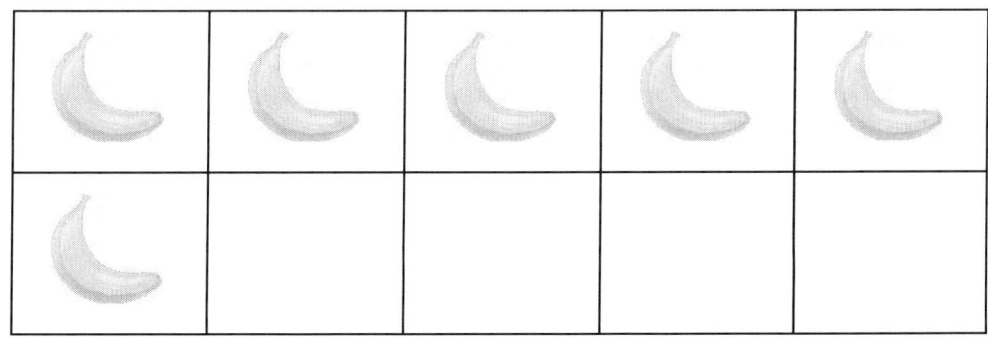

6 + ____ = 10

Writing numbers

Trace the numbers from 1 to 10.

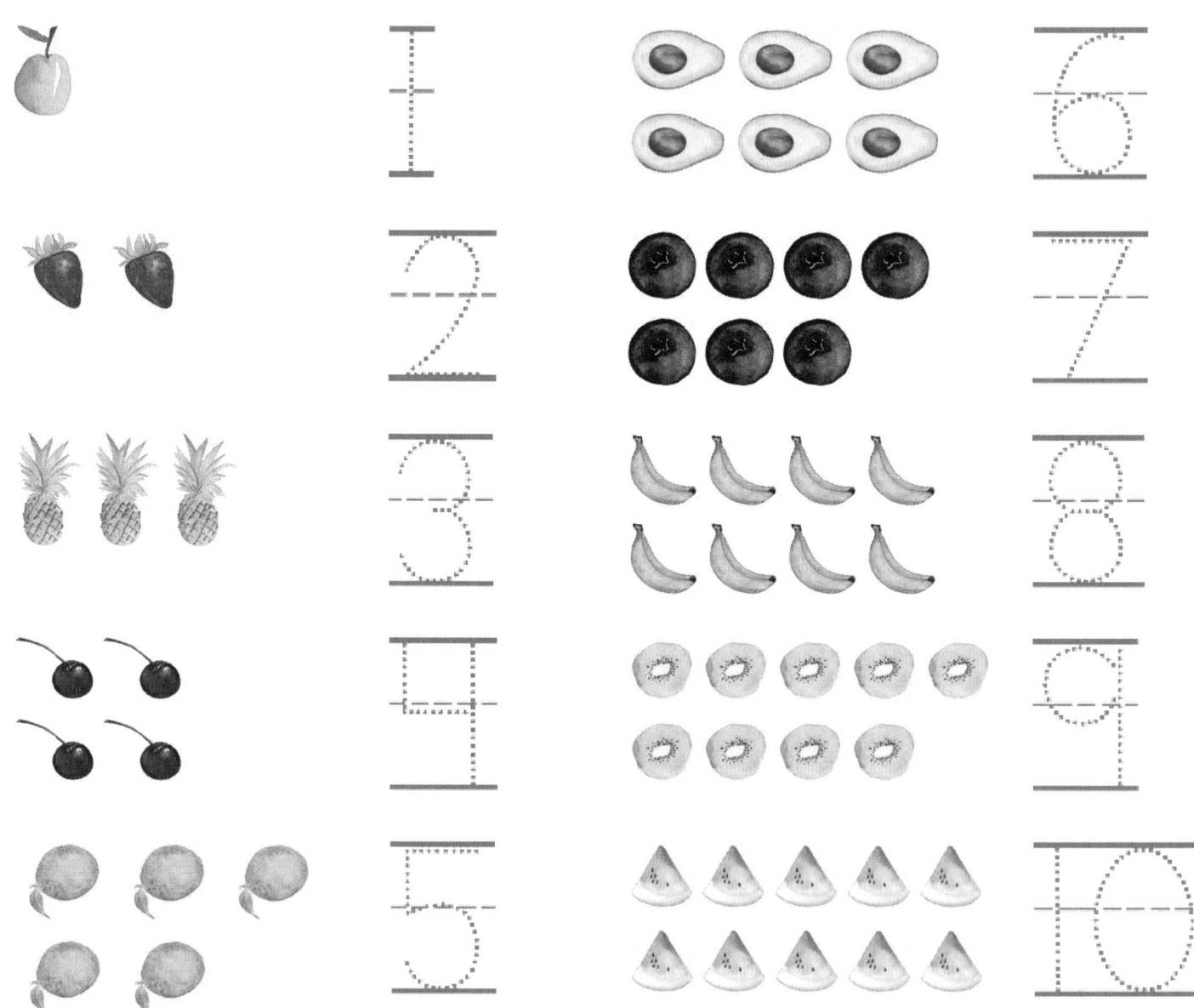

Less and more

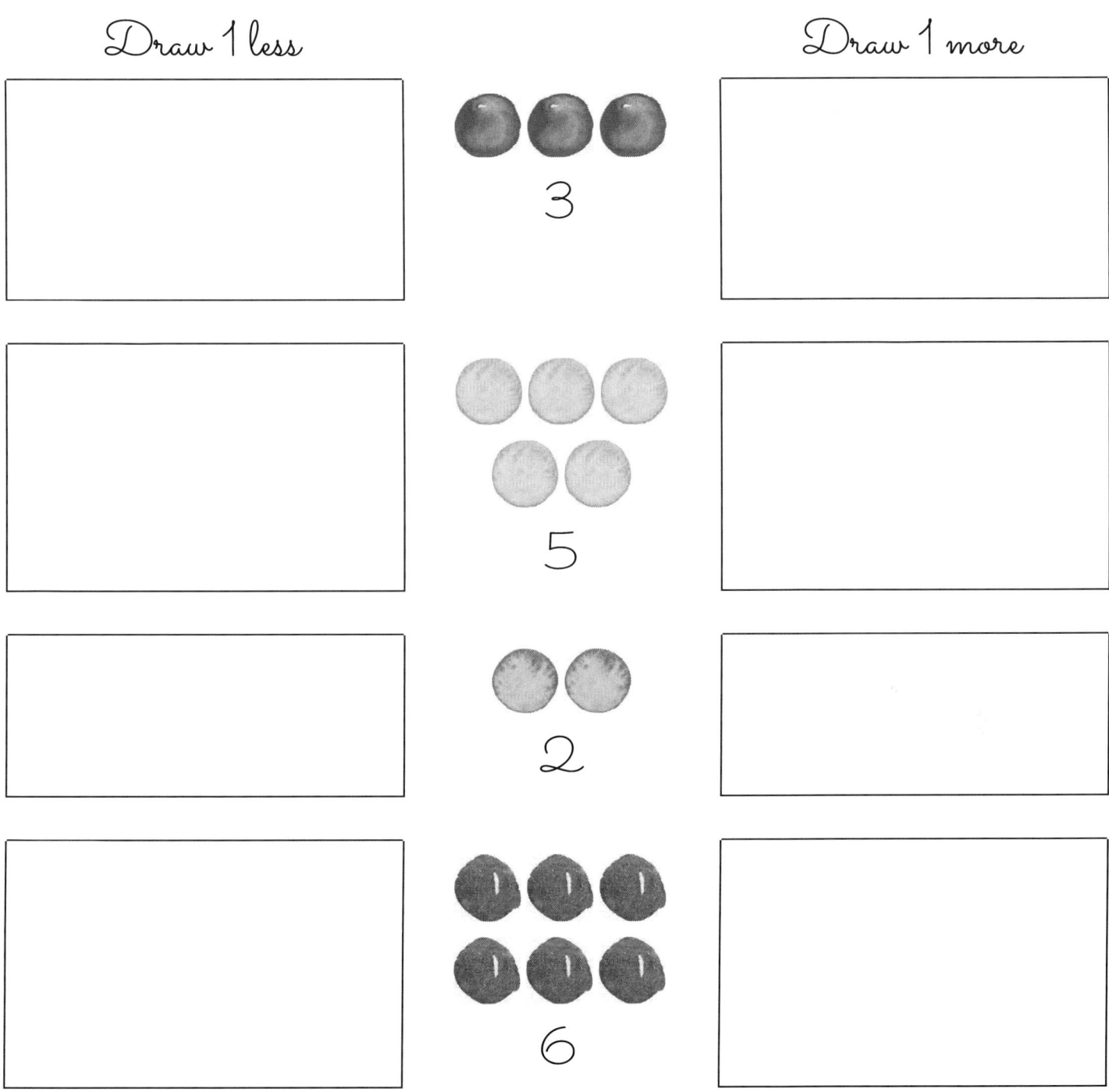

Less and more

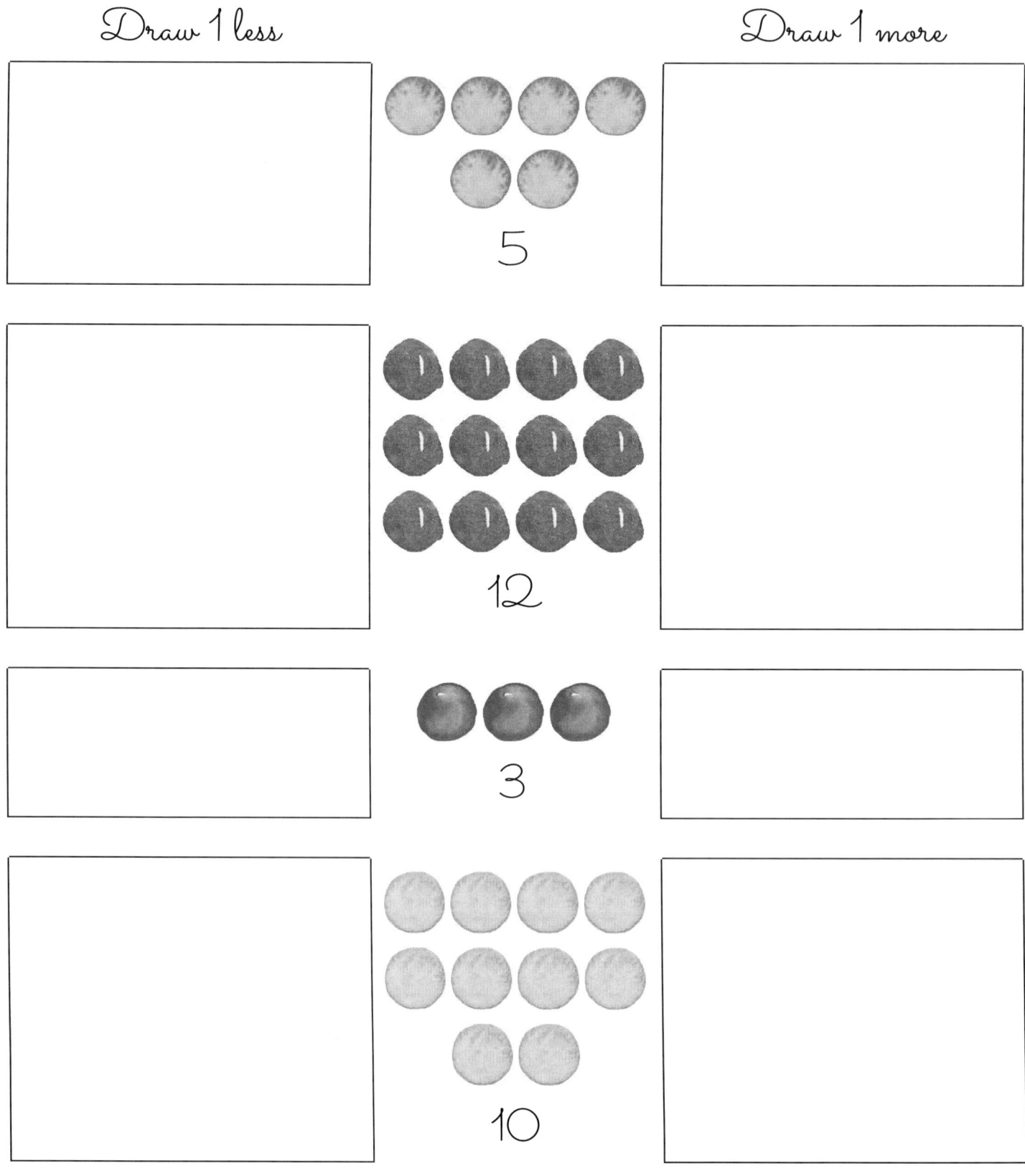

Count and circle

	1	2	3	4	5
	6	7	8	9	10

	1	2	3	4	5
	6	7	8	9	10

	1	2	3	4	5
	6	7	8	9	10

designstudioteti.etsy.com

How many can you count?

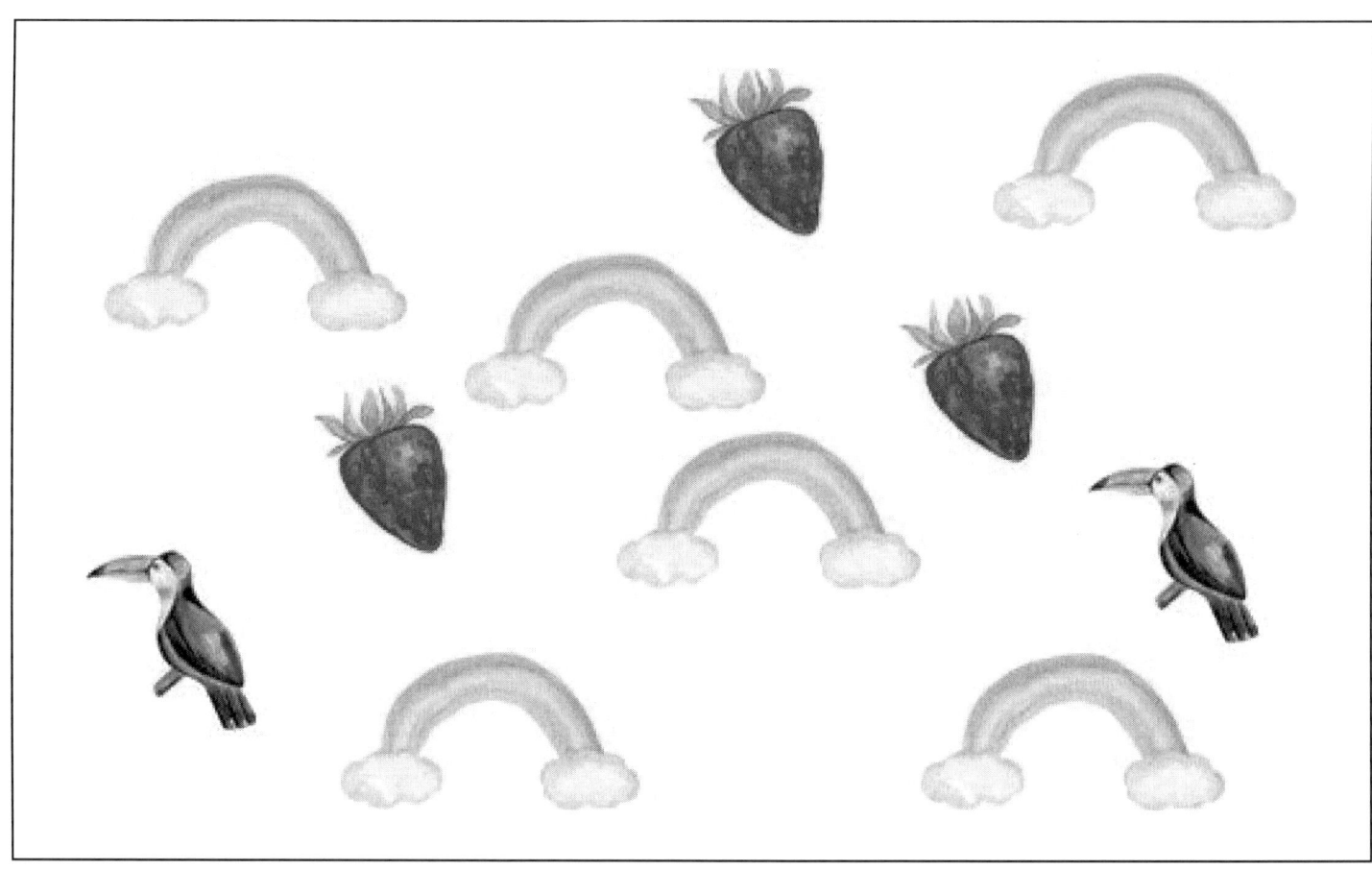

_____

_____

_____

How many can you count?

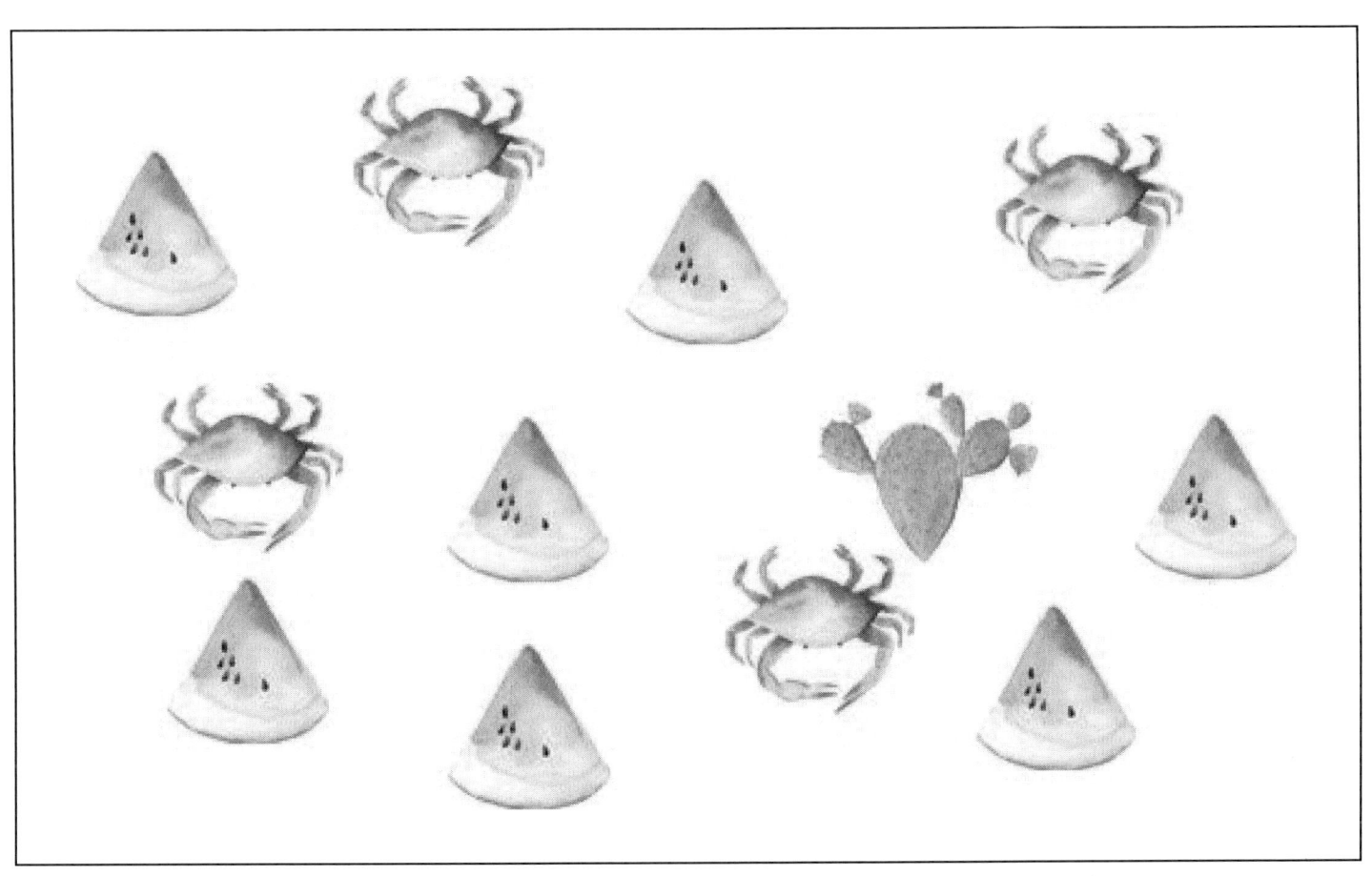

_____

_____

_____

How many can you count?

![apple] _____

![deer] _____

![popsicle] _____

designstudioteti.etsy.com

How many can you count?

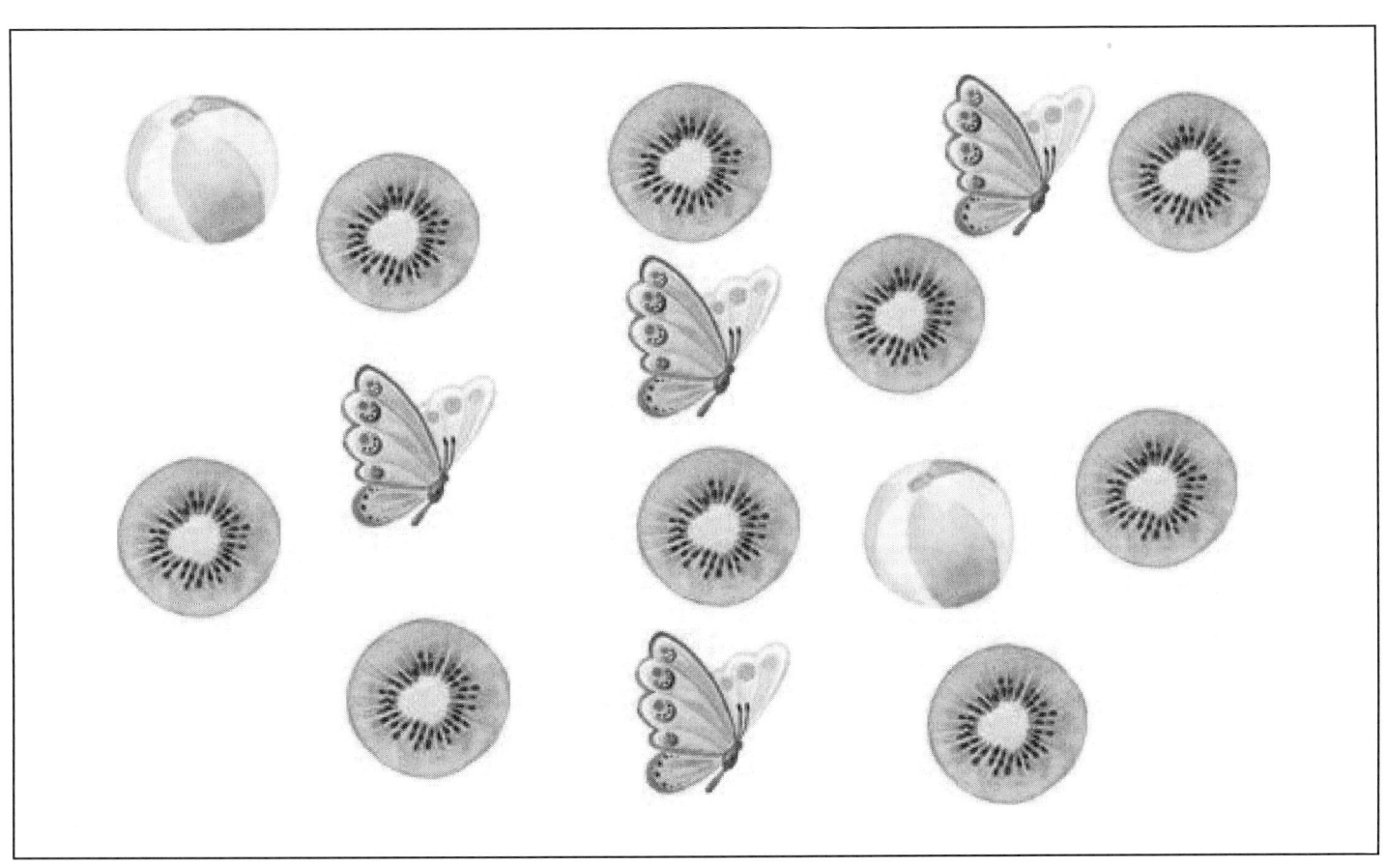

_____

_____

_____

MATH WORKSHEET
ADDING

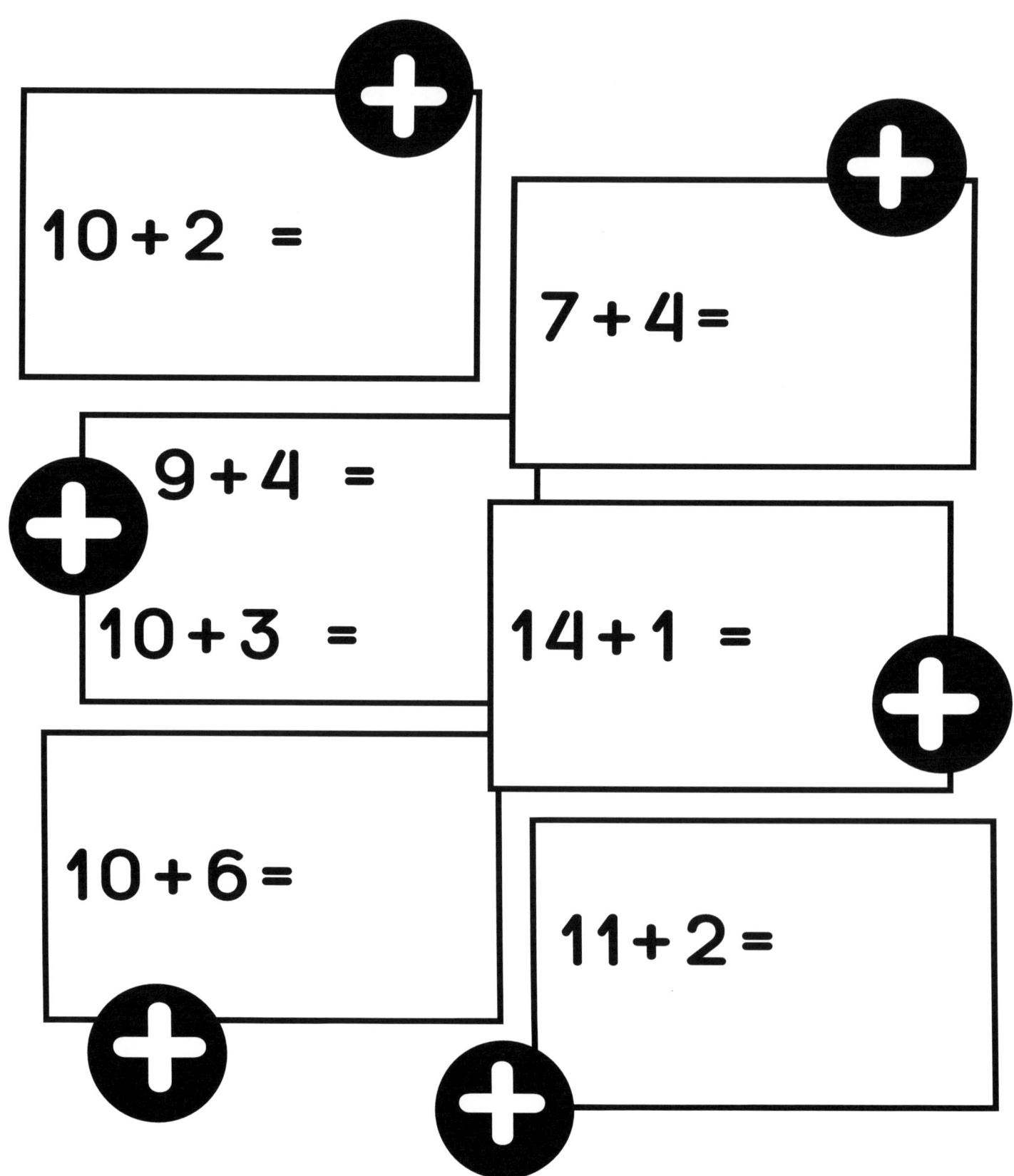

MATH WORKSHEET
ADDING

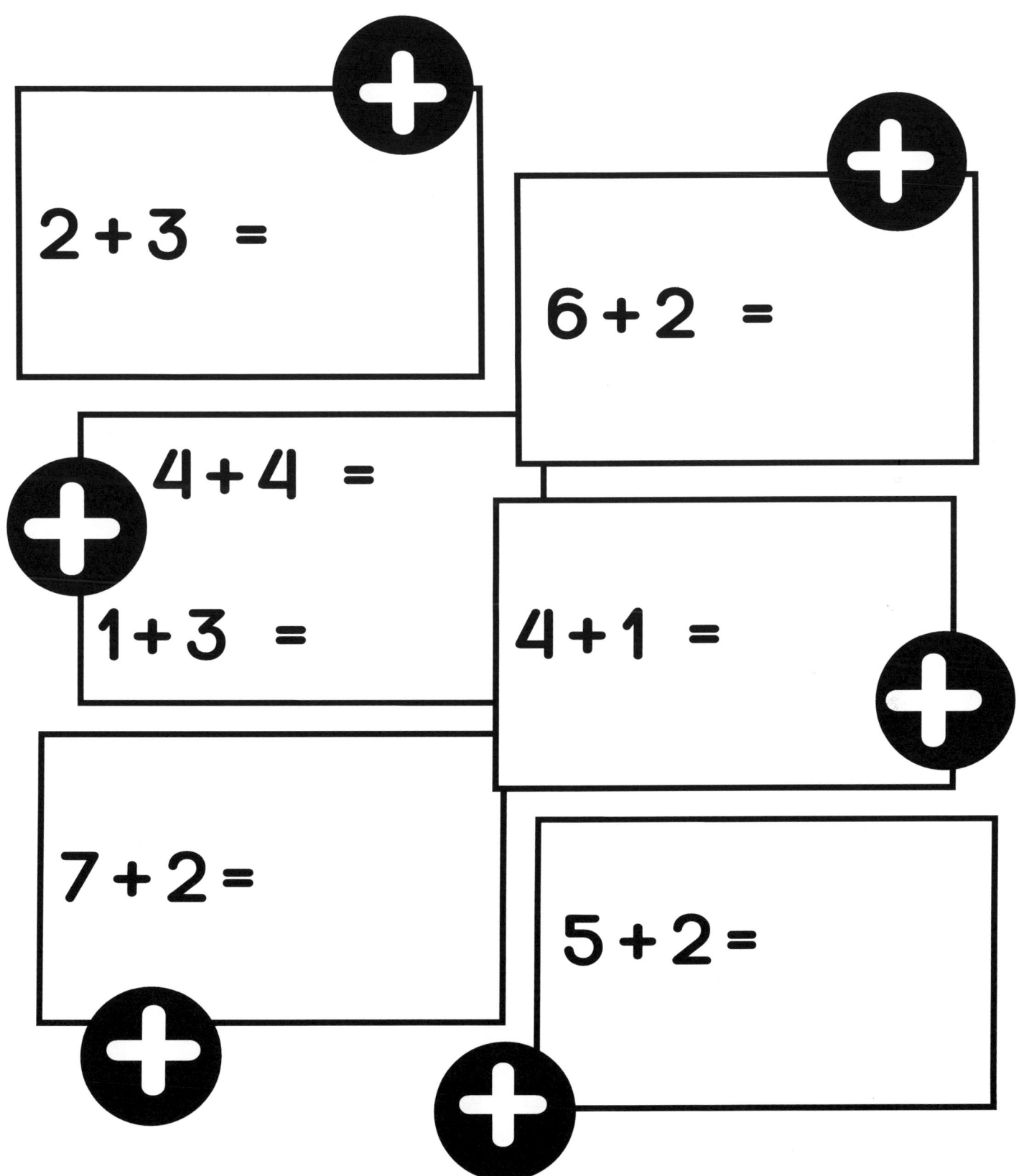

MATH WORKSHEET
ADDING

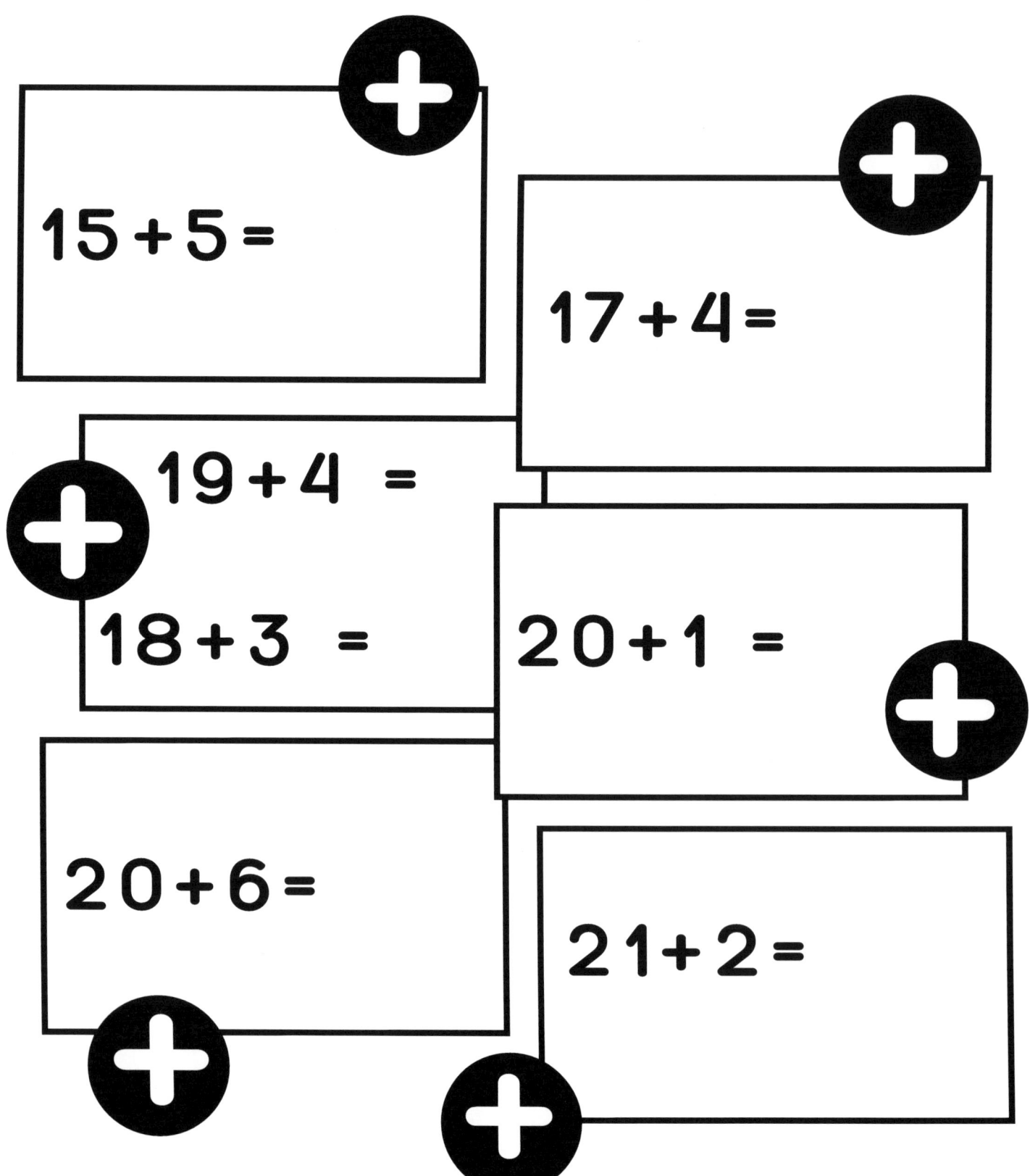

Subtract Numbers

Find the spaceship. Subtract the numbers in each box and color the spaceship with the correct answer.

6 - 3 =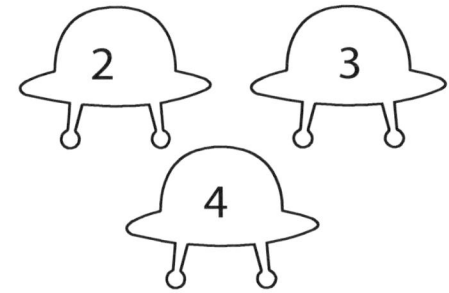

8 - 5 =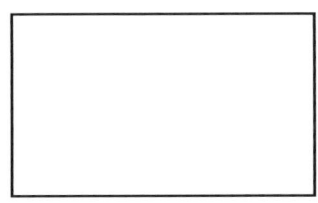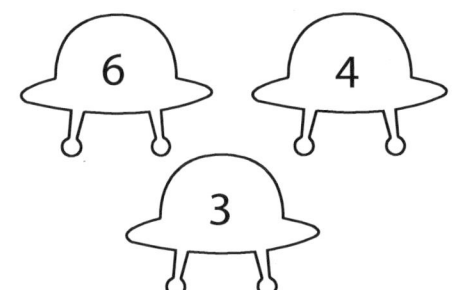

4 - 2 =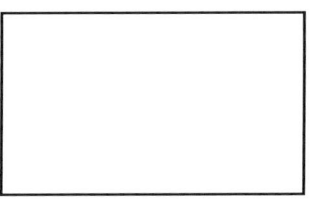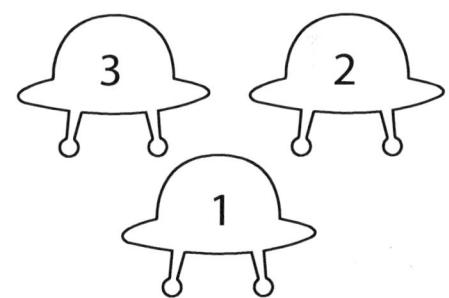

9 - 2 =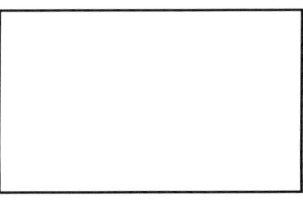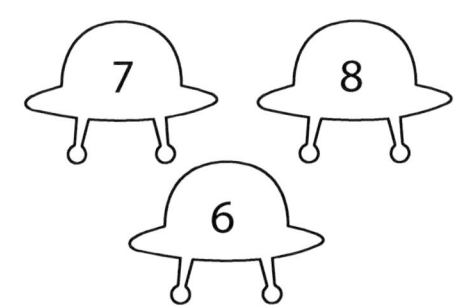

MATH WORKSHEET
SUBTRACTING

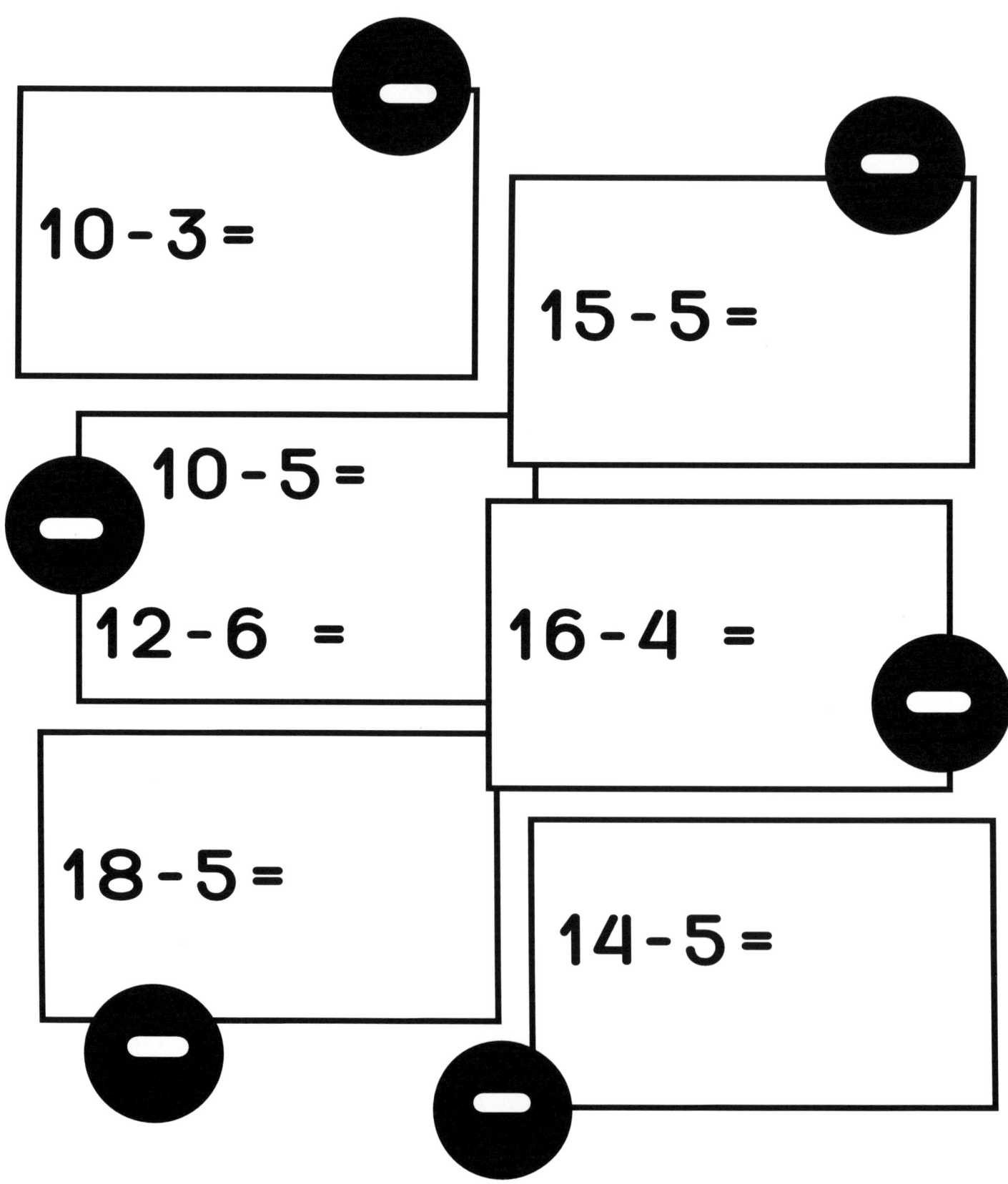

10 - 3 =

15 - 5 =

10 - 5 =

12 - 6 =

16 - 4 =

18 - 5 =

14 - 5 =

MATH WORKSHEET
SUBTRACTING

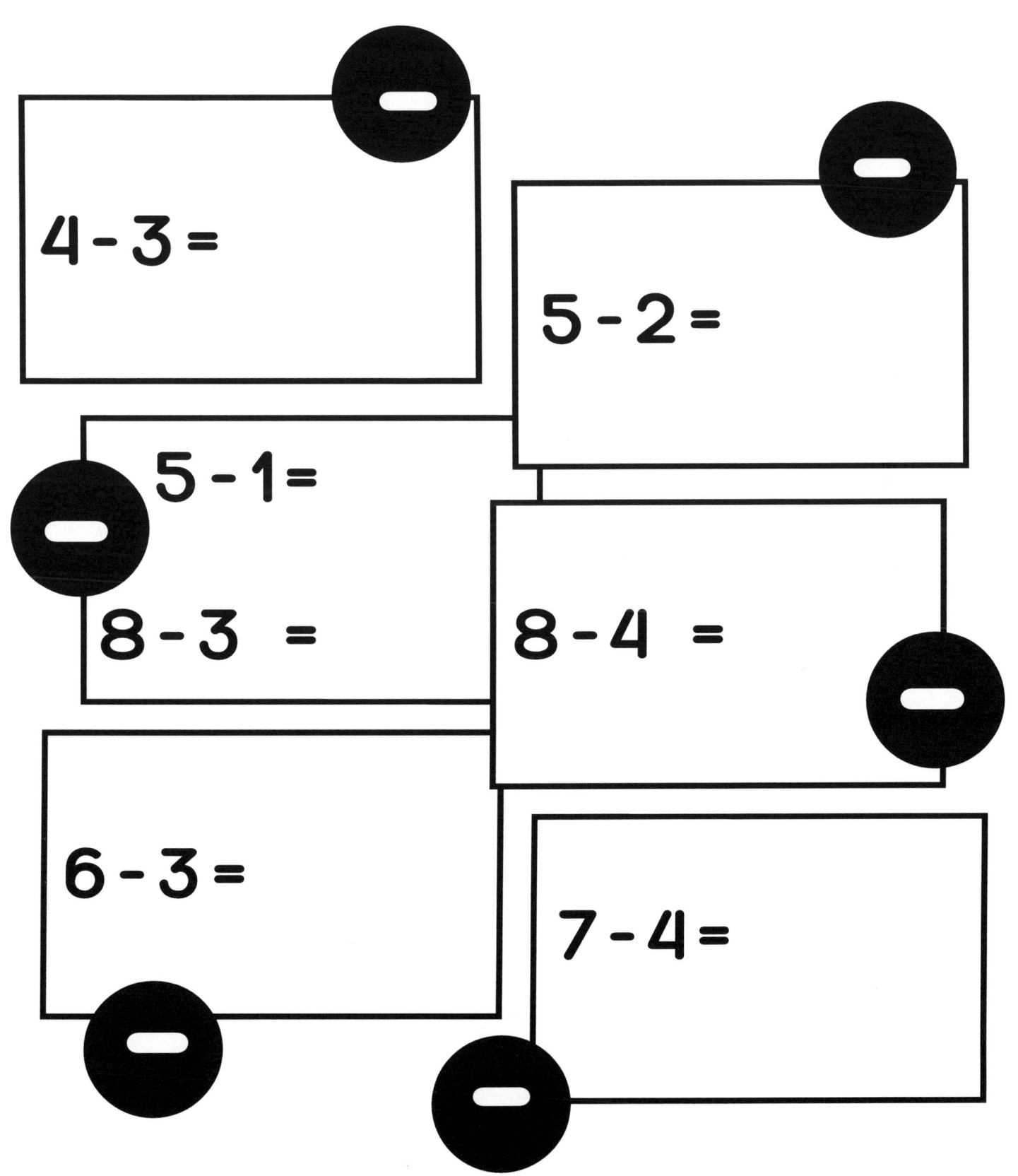

4 - 3 =

5 - 2 =

5 - 1 =

8 - 3 =

8 - 4 =

6 - 3 =

7 - 4 =

MATH WORKSHEET
SUBTRACTING

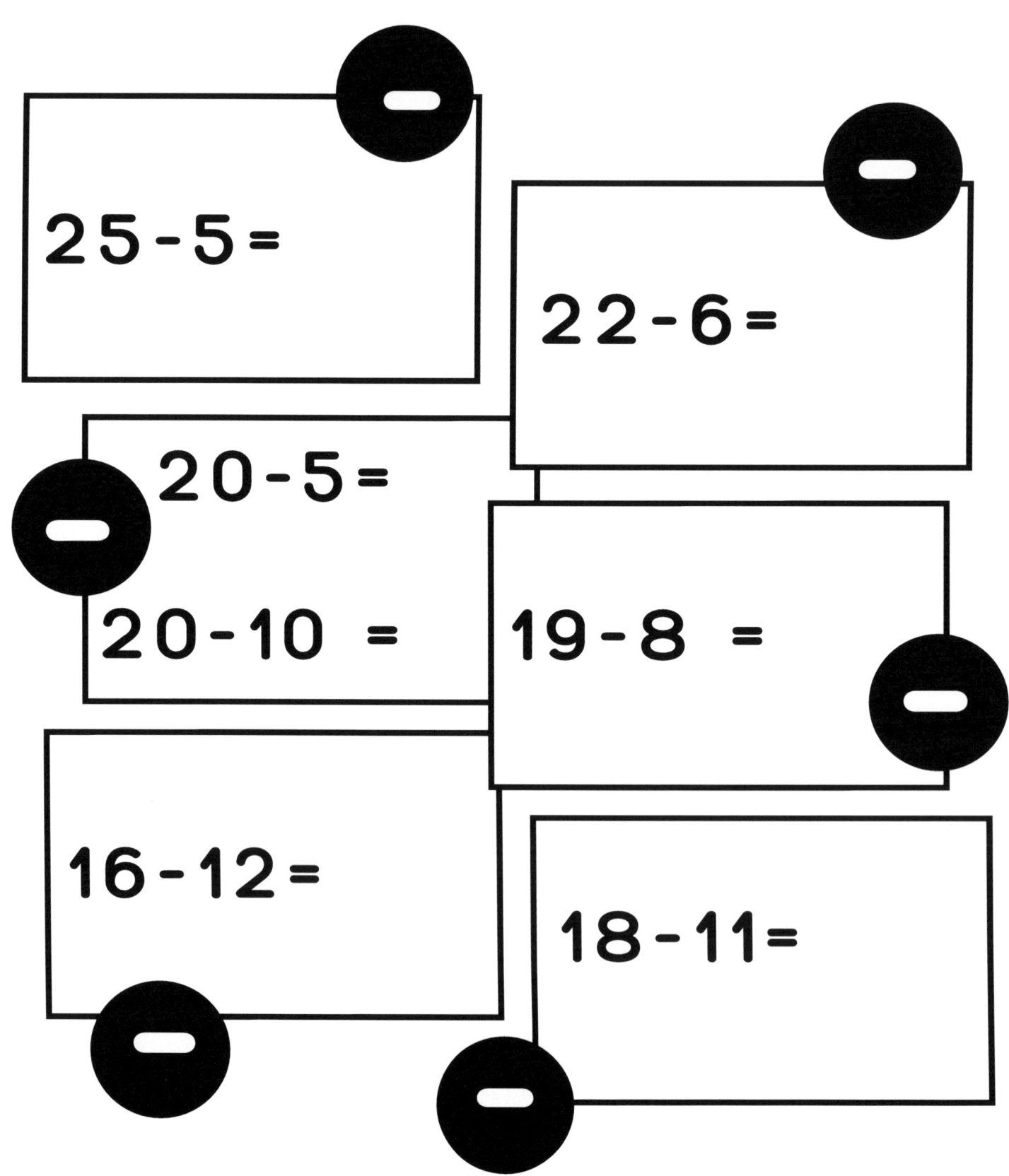

25 - 5 =

22 - 6 =

20 - 5 =

20 - 10 =

19 - 8 =

16 - 12 =

18 - 11 =

MATH WORKSHEET
WRITE THE MISSING NUMBER

Missing Numbers

Can you fill in the missing numbers by launching rocket to the space?

Half shapes

Draw a line to connect each shape with its other half.

designstudioteti.etsy.com

Half shapes

Draw a line to connect each shape with its other half.

designstudioteti.etsy.com

Match the clock

Draw a line to connect the matching times.

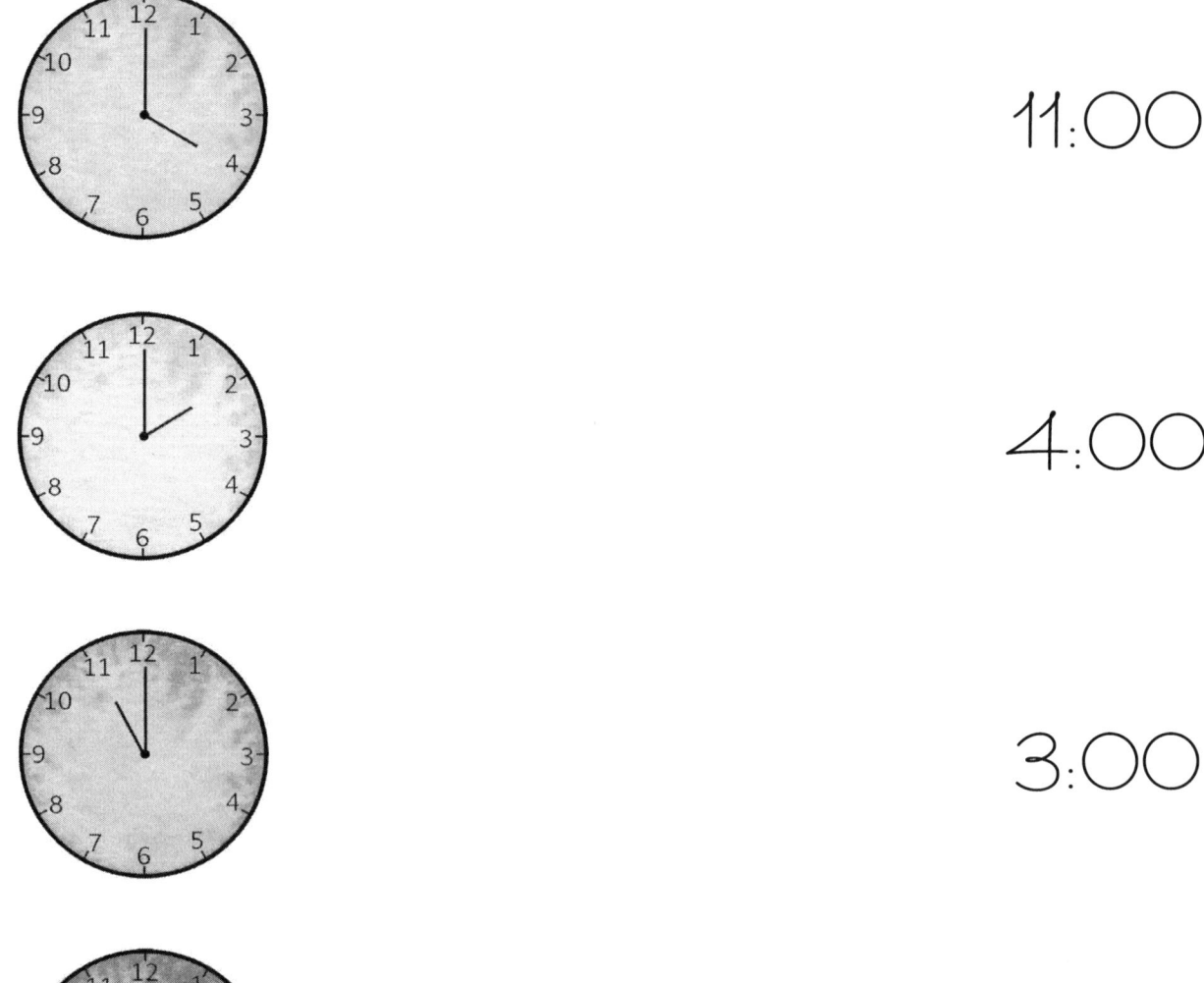

designstudioteti.etsy.com

Match the clock

Draw a line to connect the matching times.

6:00

5:00

10:00

8:00

Half pictures

Draw a line to connect each picture with its other half.

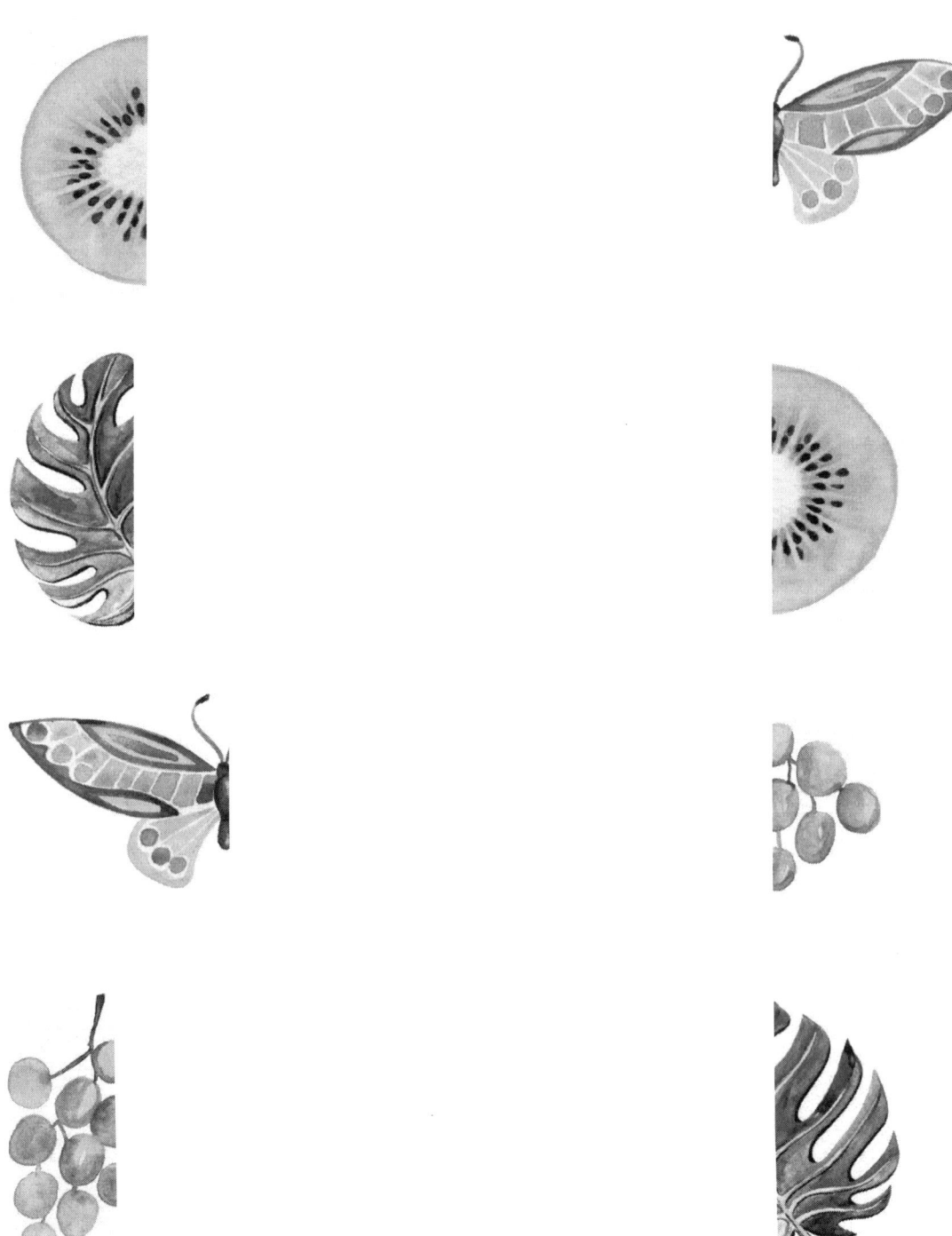

Half pictures

Draw a line to connect each picture with its other half.

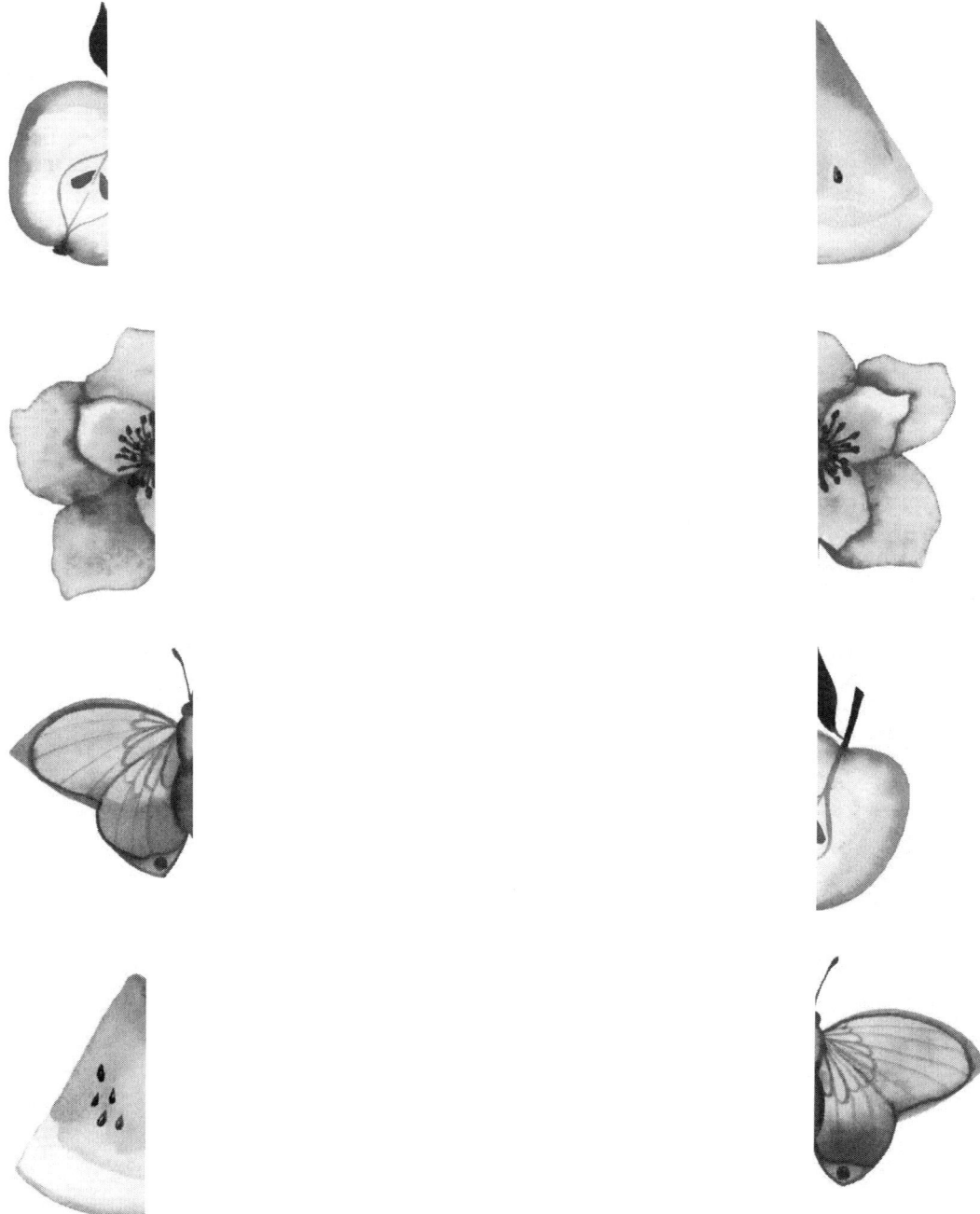

Biggest

Circle the biggest object in each row.

Smallest

Circle the smallest object in each row.

Match the Number

Draw a line from the number to the matching set of objects.

2

4

3

5

8

MATH WORKSHEET
COUNT THE OBJECTS AND WRITE THE NUMBER

Counting

Count the objects. Write the correct number in the box. Color the objects for fun.

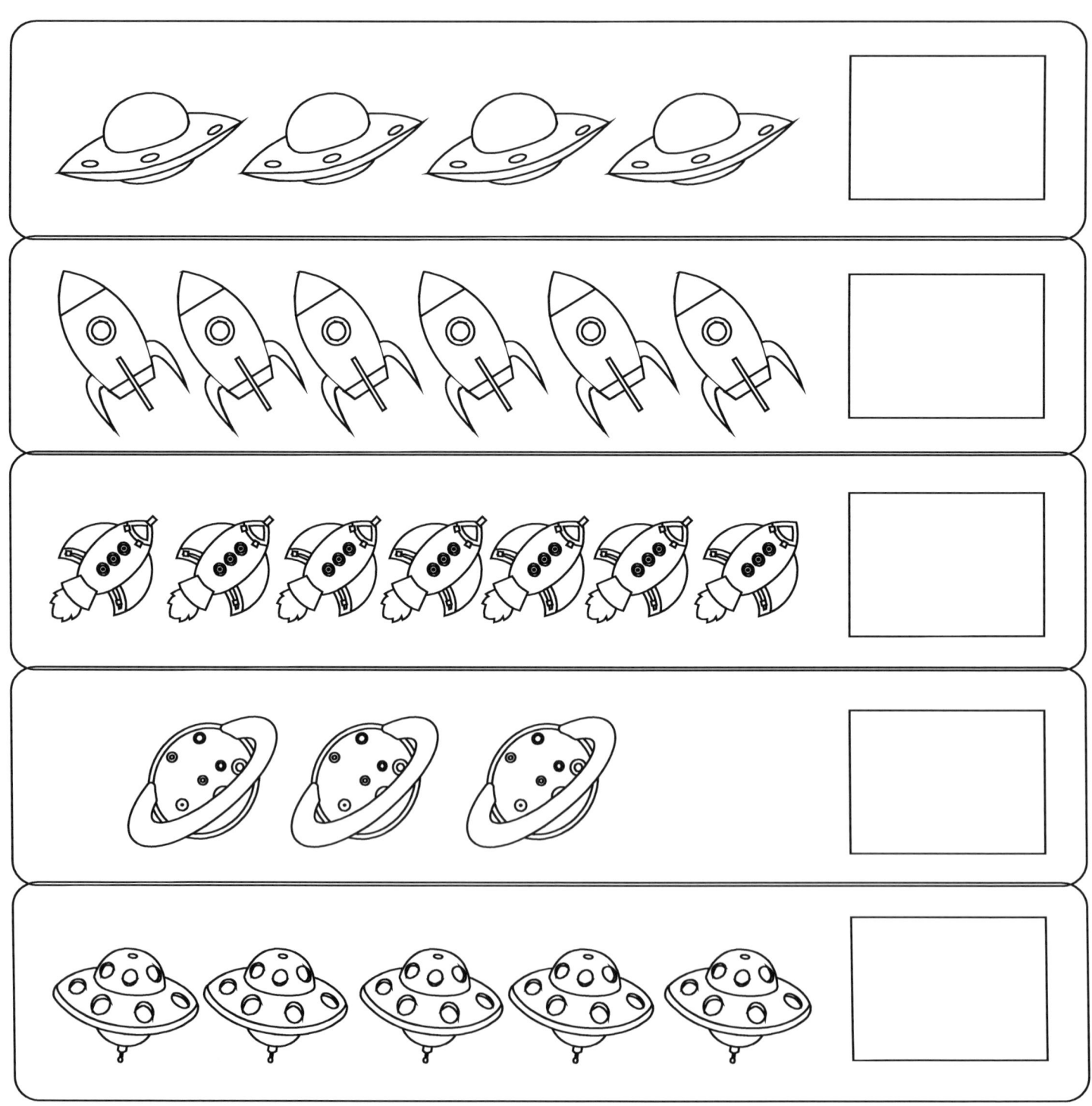

ARRANGE THE NUMBERS FROM THE SMALLEST TO THE LARGEST

7-3-5-9-7-1-2

4-6-12-2-8-0-10

9-6-15-3-12-0-18

ADDITIONS

1+1=...   1+3=...
1+2=...   1+4=...
1+2=...   1+5=...

ARRANGE THE NUMBERS FROM THE SMALLEST TO THE LARGEST

9-4-2-6-7-1-0

10-19-14-16-11-13-17

30-32-38-37-39-34-36

ADDITIONS

3+1=...   3+4=...
3+2=...   3+5=...
3+3=...   3+6=...

Printed in Great Britain
by Amazon